I Just Want *Out*

Praise for

I Just Want *Out*

"I was fortunate to receive an advanced reader copy of Jodi Schuelke's *fabulous* book, *I Just Want Out*. And I say *fabulous* because I read the whole thing in one sitting. Informative, practical, and moving, all at once, this guide will tug at your heartstrings, empower you, and hold your hand and your heart. Jodi shares her personal journey and outlines a practical and thorough step-by-step process for moving out of an emotionally abusive marriage with preparedness and integrity, so that you can move into your amazing, independent future. Bravo!"

—**Linda Bucher**, Master Certified Life Coach and Coach Mentor

"As a survivor of an emotionally and psychologically abusive relationship of 21 years, I can say this is a brilliant, step-by-step manual for those who are in the same situation and want to make the courageous choice to get out. Not only does it deal with the emotional side of this brave decision, but it tackles the practical part as well.

"When you are in an abusive relationship and you want out, the emotional overwhelm and chaos can make you forget about the practical and legal side of things. But, let me tell you, that is an essential part, as much as the emotional implications. When dealing with an abuser, you must be prepared on all fronts, because an abuser knows how to manipulate you and push your buttons.

"In sharing her story and then giving clear, practical steps, Jodi has managed to create a book that will be an indispensable part of your support system, making the ride consider ably lighter. Jodi reminds you that you're not alone!"

—**Christel Van Gelder**, Certified Life Coach, 3CHLifecoaching

"I started reading Jodi's book and got through Chapter 2 and didn't want to stop reading! I found it to be spot-on, and loved that it was written from her actual experience. I, too, went through a bad first marriage, and wish I would have found a book like this 20 years ago—the advice and pointers are awesome. It's also very encouraging for women who are nervous about leaving what they know and are used to. Love the book!"

— **Julie B.**

"*I Just Want Out* is a straightforward resource for any woman wanting to get out of their bad marriage. Jodi does an excellent job of making the reader feel they are supported and not alone during such a brave life transition. The reader gets a realistic walkthrough of the process and an organized approach to moving out of a bad situation. It's an easy read, with valuable insights!"

— **Judith P.**

"Congratulations, Jodi, for having the courage to listen to your heart, for making the admirable choice to leave a bad marriage, and now for sharing your success story with the world. There are so many nuggets of truth that resonated throughout the book. *I Just Want Out* is a true gift from the universe that can help so many women who find themselves in similar situations!"

—**Julie E. Cline**, Life Coach and Guide, My One HAPPY Life

"Thank you, Jodi, for sharing your story so openly. I firmly believe that the number of cases of emotional abuse within marriage is epidemic in our country. The difficulty comes in finding the courage to share it and finding others who can validate our experiences. You have done this beautifully in your book! I cannot wait to share it with others who are looking for additional validation."

—**Lynn Mclaughlin**, Founder & Professional Life Coach, Dand Alliance LLC

"In *I Just Want Out*, Jodi does an incredible job of describing how to differentiate between what we have been conditioned to believe and expect in an abusive relationship, and the realities of how a healthy relationship should function. Her words are raw and genuine, and empower women to grease and set the wheels in motion to get themselves into a safe and positive place. She provides the tools and draws from her own experiences to help with converting from feeling trapped and fearful to strong and empowered."

— **Kristen Genet**

"*I Just Want Out* really opened up my heart and mind to what many women deal with daily and feel there is no way of getting out of. All women have a choice, and it *does* matter. Jodi asks a great question: "What do you want for your future, and your children's?" Her phenomenal book provided answers and helped me to better understand my past experiences, and to know that they were not my fault."

— **Cindy C.**

"*I Just Want Out* provides a Framework™ for how to go about ending an emotionally abusive marriage. Jodi guides you through what to do, and when and how to do it, as you prepare for this life-changing journey."

— **Linda Brandt**

"There are going to be a lot of women who can relate to this book! If you're experiencing emotional abuse, physical abuse, or both, *I Just Want Out* provides hope. Jodi is living proof that happiness is out there— women just have to want it and have the heart to go get it. Jodi put in the hard work for a better, happier, and more successful life, and she and her kids are thriving now. Congratulations!"

— **Rebecca Casey**

"This is a great resource book for anyone struggling to leave their unhealthy marriage. Jodi not only spells out what to do emotionally, she offers ways to protect yourself financially in the event of a divorce. I found *I Just Want Out* to be a very informative read. Jodi writes clearly and pro vides concrete steps from her life experience to help women smartly prepare for getting divorced."

— Sherrie Erbs

"*I Just Want Out* is excellent. Jodi put her heart and soul into these pages! I loved the thorough steps of her FREEDOM Framework™ process. Any woman needing to get out of their marriage, but who doesn't know what to do or expect, can learn from this book. One passage from the book that really hit home was: 'You don't need a spouse to make you feel complete. A spouse, or any relationship for that matter, should be like an accessory—you're here to benefit each other.' Amen, sister!"

— Dawn Radtke

I Just Want
Out

Seven Careful Steps to
Leaving Your Emotionally
Abusive Husband

JODI SCHUELKE

NEW YORK

NASHVILLE • MELBOURNE • VANCOUVER

I Just Want *Out*
Seven Careful Steps to Leaving Your Emotionally Abusive Husband

© 2017 Jodi Schuelke

Published in New York, New York, by Morgan James Publishing in partnership with Difference Press. Morgan James is a trademark of Morgan James, LLC. www.MorganJamesPublishing.com

The Morgan James Speakers Group can bring authors to your live event. For more information or to book an event visit The Morgan James Speakers Group at www.TheMorganJamesSpeakersGroup.com.

Brand and product names are trademarks or registered trademarks of their respective owners.

ISBN 978-1-68350-232-6 paperback
ISBN 978-1-68350-233-3 eBook
ISBN 978-1-68350-234-0 hardcover
Library of Congress Control Number:
2016915365

Cover Design by:
Heidi Miller

Interior Design by:
Bonnie Bushman
The Whole Caboodle Graphic Design

Editing: Grace Kerina

Author's photo courtesy of:
J. Gonia Photography

In an effort to support local communities, raise awareness and funds, Morgan James Publishing donates a percentage of all book sales for the life of each book to Habitat for Humanity Peninsula and Greater Williamsburg.

Get involved today! Visit
www.MorganJamesBuilds.com

Disclaimer

The author is not a licensed professional. The information in this book does not constitute legal, medical, mental health or financial advice and should not be used as a substitute. All decisions about your personal situation (and/or your children) should be made in consultation with a licensed attorney, physician, therapist or counselor, or financial advisor. The author is not responsible for any adverse effects or consequences resulting from the application of any of the advice, practices, or procedures described herein.

This book details the author's personal experiences and opinions. Among other things, it includes the author's reactions and memories. The author acknowledges that others may remember certain situations that she recounts in the book differently than she does. She is aware that others may have experienced some of the situations in this book in a way that is significantly different from the way she portrays them. In order to maintain their anonymity, identifying characteristics and details such as names, physical properties, occupations and places of residence have been either changed or omitted.

Dedication

To Alec and Ethan, for enduring this journey along with me, and for showing me every day that it was worth it.

To my husband, Dan, for always believing in me and my wild and adventurous dreams, and for his constant encouragement and support.

Table of Contents

Introduction

If you've picked up this book, it's my hunch you're feeling exhausted from having worked so hard to make your marriage better and to truly feel happy. You've longed to feel respected, supported, and unconditionally loved. Instead you've had to carefully watch each step you take.

You've experienced challenges and pushback, had your heart stepped on, and your hopes blown to bits. You've taken on all the major responsibilities of managing the household, being the primary caretaker of the children, plus holding down a challenging job. Your contributions go unnoticed and you're criticized for not doing more, or doing things more perfectly, and for every minor flaw you possess. When problems arise or things fall apart which are not your fault, you are blamed and expected to fix the mess. And, if there are successes, the accomplishment and glory is stolen and becomes his.

Yet you've soldiered on, and over the years figured out workarounds to avoid his negative reactions and learned to quickly hand over appreciation for all the hard work to him. You pretend to the outside world that everything is fine, while inside you feel defeated, ashamed, and resentful.

Being a soldier means you have been expected to hold it together, never outwardly disrespecting the commander, and you keep working hard, despite the horrible conditions. You've climbed the ranks into parenthood and now have others who you're responsible for and who you're unwilling to sacrifice for a cause that doesn't feel worth it anymore.

What you're fighting for are the rights and freedom for yourself and your children. Your battlefront is at home. The enemy is not an outsider—it's the commander, your husband.

The Cost of Staying

There are risks involved in both staying and leaving your marriage. None of which should be taken lightly. Imagine for a moment what your life might look like in the future if you stay. Close your eyes and fast-forward five years.

First, envision your husband. Has anything changed for the better, or has it gotten worse? What is his behavior like at home and at work? How is he treating the children? What's their relationship with him like? Is he spending wildly, or are there hints that he's having an affair— emotional or physical? Has he supported any of your or your children's wishes, goals, or dreams? Write down what you see in your mind's eye.

Next, I invite you to envision your children. Again, look ahead five years from now. What might they be like? What are their behaviors? What does their relationship look like with their dad, and also with you? Are they being consistently criticized and yelled at? Are they displaying similar behaviors as their dad? How are they treating you—respectfully or disrespectfully? How are they interacting with their friends and other relatives? How are they doing in school, and are they having behavioral problems there? Are they happy or stressed? When do they display either of those emotions? Jot down your answers for each child.

Now look ahead at yourself. Who are you in five years? How do you feel? Are you happy and content, or miser able? Are you still pretending to the outside world that everything is just fine? How is your personal life affecting your job and your happiness with your career? How do you look physically? Have you gained (or lost) weight? Do you look haggard and a lot older than someone your age? Are you healthy and managing your stress appropriately, or are you dealing with stress-induced health issues? Are you on anti-depressants or anti-anxiety meds? Write all of that down as well.

Read through everything you wrote down. How does your future look? Good? Or pretty bleak? I suspect the latter. Based on your answers, I have a hunch you can already see that it'll cost far more than you ever imagined if you choose to stay. Staying equals sacrificing your and your children's emotional well-being, potential to have healthy relationships in the future, and a truly happy and fulfilling life.

The Benefits of Leaving

Choosing to leave your marriage will be the beginning of a beautiful transformation for you and your children—it's a gift!

Imagine a life where you can feel free to be fully yourself. You have free time, emotional and physical space to create the life you want, and you offer your children better opportunities. You start anew and are able to pursue any of your goals and dreams. You are free of having to answer to anyone, ask for their permission, or try to persuade them to see the benefits in what you want to do. Gone will be the daily stress ors of carefully watching every footstep (your own and your children's) to avoid stepping on a landmine, because there will be none, and you'll be able to breathe easy.

Life will be so much better when your only regret was that you didn't leave years sooner!

But You're Afraid

I understand that you may be feeling that you did something wrong to allow this to have happened and that it's your fault. You may worry that you won't have any support, that nobody will believe you or stand by your side and help you. You may have doubts that you could pull this off, that he won't ever let you leave, or let you have the kids or any of your belongings. You may think you won't be able to support yourself, or feel fearful of what others might think of you. And you may even have a sick feeling in your stomach from worrying that your children will hate you.

Sweetheart, I totally get it. Every fear you have, I had too. What you've endured is not your fault. It's not all in your head, and *you are absolutely not crazy*. Your husband may want you to believe he's all you've got and you'd never be able to make it on your own, but that's untrue. There is nothing wrong with wanting to leave your marriage and have a better life. Your children will adjust to the change and be better off in the long run.

Fear is a natural instinct and is intended to keep us safe, but when you hide behind fear versus utilizing it as a catalyst for change, you'll stay stuck and miserable. You are a soldier and a survivor. You are smart and you *can* do this.

I Will Show You the Way

This book chronicles my awakening—how I planned for my and my children's departure, and how we safely and successfully left my emotionally abusive first marriage. Any mistakes and missteps I experienced along the way are also shared, which I hope will help you better navigate the process so you can get out safely and swiftly.

I've also included information and tips from clients I've coached and those I interviewed who also left an abusive marriage, as well as insight from legal professionals. My wish is that this book will help you cross over to a better and healthier life, and a more promising future for yourself and your children.

What Lies Ahead

In *I Just Want Out*, I will use my journey to freedom to illustrate the seven steps of The FREEDOM Framework™ process, so that you can safely and smartly leave your emotionally abusive marriage. I also provide a general overview of the divorce process in the United States.

Please use caution: This is not a book to leave lying around or on display for all to see.

Chapter 1
The Slow Awakening

When I Knew

It was Saturday, October 17, 1998, at approximately 1:15 p.m., and I'd just delivered my second son. When the doctor handed him to me I experienced what no mother ever wants to experience, let alone admit—I'd made a huge mistake. The mistake wasn't my newborn son. Absolutely not! I fell in love with him the second I knew I was pregnant. The mistake was the *reason* I chose to get pregnant, because I was hoping it would improve my marriage.

I sat there holding my newborn son, feeling so proud, but also in a state of surreal shock and seeing visions of myself in the future as a single mom with my two boys. That vision had never occurred to me before, and yet I didn't feel afraid about how drastically our future was going to change.

He Loves Me

I grew up in a rural area of east central Wisconsin and attended a small high school where everyone pretty much knew one another. I was the fourth of five kids in my family and spent lots of time around my older siblings' friends when they came over to hang out.

I met Rich (not his real name) in the fall of 1987, when I was 15 years old, during my sophomore year of high school. It was a typical Friday night and I was cruising around town with my friend Jill and her boyfriend. We pulled into the local grocery store parking lot next to two guys blaring '80s rock music from their car stereo. I knew one of the guys, Steve—he was a friend of my older brother—but not the other guy. Steve introduced me and Jill to his friend Rich. Both Steve and Rich had graduated in May, had cars, and liked to party. We decided the five of us would hang out for the night and we all piled into Steve's car to cruise around and drink.

I thought Rich was really cool and he acted so mature, which made him seem really attractive to me too. He had a full-time job and lived alone with his older brother, who was 21 and could buy beer. Rich's house, as I had heard previously from my older siblings, was one of the main party hangouts in town.

We all had fun hanging out that night, and when it was time for me to go home I asked Rich if he'd drive me back. I lived ten miles away, and he quickly agreed. We started dating a couple of weeks later and things quickly got serious between us. He'd regularly pick me up after school and drive me home or to work. Our circle of friends included people from his age group all the way down to mine.

There wasn't much to do where we lived, so most times we hung out watching VHS movies or went out with friends. Rich was very sweet and seemed attentive to me, which made me feel special. The other bonus was that my family liked him too. Everything seemed perfect because he loved me.

Ignoring the Signs

The signs were there all along, but I didn't want to see them. Rich was the youngest of three boys who had been raised by their single mother (who I learned a few years into our relationship was diagnosed as paranoid schizophrenic) and a widowed grandmother. Their dad had abandoned the family when Rich was a year old. The eldest brother lived in Arizona and worked as a teacher. Rich's childhood had been very tough, and he'd had only a few occasional adult male role models in his life.

After Rich and I had been dating four months, his brother, Tom, who Rich lived with, committed suicide at a friend's house. Rich had stayed late watching a movie at my house that night, and when he got home he was visited by the police and informed of what had happened to his brother.

The next morning when Rich called, he was very robotic in his speaking, like he was still in shock. I could tell he had been crying, but he kept it together over the phone. I shared the news with my mom and told her that I didn't know what to do. I had not experienced deaths other than elderly relatives who died of natural causes and a couple from our church who lost their infant to SIDS. I had no idea how to process Tom's suicide, let alone be supportive to Rich. Mom replied by saying, "All you can do is be there for him."

Things quickly changed with Rich following Tom's death. He wanted to spend all of his free time with me, which I was fine with because I wanted to be there for him. When we were alone he began to reveal his anger and started putting me down. In one instance, he got pissed when I told him I was going to buy a new waterbed with the money I had saved up, saying that was stupid and I'd be blowing my money. I felt hurt and confused as to what happened to my sweet boyfriend. But when I talked to my parents or friends about it they all said he was still grieving, that it would take time, and to be patient. I was 15 years old, naïve, and in love, so I stuck by him.

By the following year, Rich seemed to be out of his funk and back to having fun. I was involved in choir and basketball and had a part-time job at a local restaurant, so I had lots going on in addition to my schoolwork. I had saved enough money to buy a car and was able to drive myself and feel more independent. Rich's only request was that I call and check in with him after I got home. I thought he was being thoughtful because he loved me, but the first time I forgot to call, Rich called to yell at me for making him worry. I felt bad that I had forgotten, but I really didn't like it when he got angry with me, so I made sure it didn't happen again.

I had occasional thoughts of wanting to break up with him, but mostly only if we had a big fight. All of our coupled friends seemed to get along really well and I felt ashamed when Rich and I fought and didn't want anyone to know. He always blamed me, even when the issue was his fault, but usually a few days later he'd give me a gift as his way of apologizing. I was so naïve and had no clue what was happening to me.

It was very common where I was from for girls to have long-term boyfriends, starting in high school, and then marry them later and start a family. Girls who broke up with their long-term boyfriends were usually cast out of the friend circle. I loved my boyfriend and also didn't want to lose my friends.

By my senior year I had given up basketball because I really wasn't that good a player and I grew tired of being asked why my boyfriend never came to my games. As the year progressed and I started looking at colleges, Rich used a variety of ploys to keep me from going away. First, he said I wasn't smart enough because I had a mid-level GPA and hadn't scored very high on my ACT exam. His second attempt focused on all the student loan debt I'd be stuck with. The final push was threatening that our relationship wouldn't last if I went away to school, and that he wouldn't spend the gas money to come see me. I was terrified of losing him and settled on attending a local community college so we could still see each other every day.

By my second year of college, we were living together in his apartment. Within a few months, he proposed, saying it seemed like the next logical step. I was in love with the idea of a wedding and getting married, but I had no clue about what it was going to be like on the other side of that commitment.

Cold Feet

Ours was a whirlwind engagement, filled with tons of wedding plans; I was the first of my siblings to get married and my parents wanted a big celebration. I was also juggling school and work, as well as my fiancé's growing, suffocating control. As soon as I began living under his roof, I was not allowed to call family or friends long-distance, and if they called me he limited the amount of time I could be on the phone. I could only hang out with our local friend circle and wasn't allowed to participate in any college activities.

On my graduation day he conveniently picked a fight with me and refused to attend the ceremony, so I went alone with my parents.

All of his craziness was getting out of hand, so two weeks before our wedding I wanted to call it off. I went to tell my parents, who proceeded to talk me out of it, saying it was pre-wedding jitters. They pointed out that we had so much money invested already, and mentioned the shame and embarrassment that would ensue. I didn't want to disappoint them, so I accepted that it was probably only the jitters.

We went through with the big, fancy wedding and our honeymoon to Disney World. I was blissfully miserable.

Husbandry 101

We had been married less than a year. The more adult responsibilities crept into the picture, the more I saw Rich not handling things well. He was easily stressed. He pushed back against any change that was out of his control. And he preferred following his set routines. I was expected to tow the line with what he wanted, and when I didn't or pushed back a huge argument erupted.

That certainly was not how I had imagined our marriage was going to be. I felt ashamed to tell anyone how unhappy I was. All of our married friends seemed happy and assumed we were too. I didn't think anyone would ever believe how messed up things were, because Rich acted so different around other people. I had heard many older married people say that marriage was a lot of work. I'd grown up watching my dad bend over backwards trying to fix things if my parents had a fight or if my mom got upset with him.

By then I'd convinced myself that Rich didn't know *how* to be a good husband, because of the way he'd been raised. I felt a responsibility to him because of all the time we'd been together. I had heard countless times from other women that they had to "teach" their men how to be husbands, so that's what I tried to do too.

Disasters In Matrimony

We both had full-time jobs. Rich worked in a factory as a machine operator and I worked in an office doing data entry. He complained about his job a lot, but wasn't willing to search for anything else. Then, one day, he called saying he'd quit his job. That news felt like a kick in the stomach. We were barely getting by on our two salaries, and suddenly it all fell on me to support us.

Rich decided to go to school to learn about computers, and did very well in his classes. A semester away from earning his associate's degree, he decided to drop out because he was sick of school. I was so upset. He had just limited his future employment opportunities in that field and the potential for extra income. He had more than enough credits for a certificate, so I pushed him to get it so he had something official to offer when he applied for jobs.

He landed an entry-level job as a network administrator and seemed to really like it. When Rich was happy our relationship seemed better.

The Drunken Pregnancy

Three years into our marriage, I started to get the baby itch. We'd had lots of distractions with other family and friends getting married or having kids, and I was getting questioned about when we would have a baby.

He wasn't too keen on the idea, at first, saying kids cost lots of money and that he wanted to travel before we had kids. After a few months, he finally agreed and I got pregnant. I assumed his agreement was a sign that he was finally learning how to be a husband.

My first trimester was very exhausting and I slept all the time. When I wasn't sleeping I felt nauseated if I didn't eat every couple of hours, which quickly led me to gain weight. My husband complained about this change in me and within a few weeks began drinking in the evenings. First it was only a beer or two with dinner, then it increased to a twelve-pack a night. When I expressed my concerns about his drinking problem, he denied it and said he could do whatever he wanted. This continued throughout my pregnancy.

When I was a couple of weeks from my due date, I'd had enough. I was furious and gave him an ultimatum: "Either you stop drinking or I'm leaving and I'll raise our child alone." That did it, and he stopped drinking.

We welcomed the birth of our first child, Adam (not his real name), in March of 1995. Adam was the first grandchild on both sides of the family and everyone was excited to meet him. The visitors and new baby excitement were a welcome distraction from the drinking drama. Adam was a good baby and started sleeping through the night within only a couple of months, which helped make being a newbie parent feel pretty easy.

With the birth of our son we were nearing the four-year mark of being married. Rich and I had good stretches that lasted as long as a couple of months, and I was convinced having a baby had been all that was needed for Rich to finally change. He really enjoyed being a dad and he loved our son.

Trying To Better Our Situation

I returned to college when Adam was seven months old to pursue a bachelor's degree in business management. My employer offered tuition reimbursement and the rest was covered by financial aid. The program was an accelerated adult degree program with classes one night a week. Rich didn't like the idea of me going back to school, because of the student loans and my being gone all evening sometimes. I found myself having to convince him that I was going back to school so we could have a better future.

By then I had worked in the insurance industry for a few years but was hitting the glass ceiling. I needed the bachelor's degree to get a better-paying position. Rich reluctantly agreed and stayed home with Adam while I was away at class.

I learned really fast that if I had homework I'd avoid an argument and being called selfish if I completed it at work or in the evening after Adam went to bed. I struggled with a statistics class early on in the program, missing a B letter grade by only a few points. Rich called me stupid when I told him my grade and said he knew it would be a waste of money letting me go to college. I got the sense he wanted me to fail at school, which made me angry. I knew I wasn't stupid and was determined to prove him wrong.

Between working 32 hours a week, going to school, studying, and taking care of our baby and the house, I was exhausted. Rich made dinner every night and took care of Adam when I was gone to class, but wouldn't help with anything else.

A few months after I started school I noticed that Rich had started drinking again and not hiding that he was buying twelve-packs of beer. There was no way I was going to watch this replay, so I gave him the ultimatum again: either he stopped drinking immediately or I was leaving with Adam. He didn't believe me. When he came home the next night with beer in tow I gathered up Adam and we left and went to my parents'.

Rich was livid with me for leaving and for involving my parents, but I didn't care. He called to yell at me and demand I bring his son home, but I refused. He drove out to my parents', yelled at me in front of them, managed to take Adam from me, and left.

My parents were very shaken up by Rich's intimidating behavior and told me I'd better go home and make sure my son was okay. I was so angry that he'd started drinking again, humiliated by the way he'd treated me, and embarrassed that my parents had to witness all that. I sobbed all the way home. I knew he wouldn't harm our son, but I was very tired of how he'd been behaving, and I desperately wanted him to change.

When I talked to my parents the next day, they asked if Rich had settled down and if we had made up yet. My heart was crushed because, in that instance, I believed they thought it was my fault. I lied to them and said everything was fine. In reality, I had been tiptoeing around what had happened at home, letting Rich cool off, and trying to focus my energy on taking care of Adam, school, and my job. Things returned to normal within a few weeks.

First Family Vacation

During the good times, it was easy to make plans to do house projects, make larger purchases, or plan fun activities. We both wanted to take a vacation and finally had extra money from our last tax return.

Our first family vacation was driving out to Yellowstone National Park. We visited Mount Rushmore, the Badlands, and the Corn Palace along the way, and we stayed in Cody, Wyoming. We really enjoyed our trip, for the most part. But the good times never lasted long.

On our last night in Wyoming, Rich had a fit when I wanted him to take Adam swimming while I ran out to do some souvenir shopping. I had to wait until the next day and was only allowed 15 minutes to shop before we hit the interstate. I was very frustrated that he was making me rush when there was no hurry to leave. My mood triggered Rich to decide we were going to drive straight home to Wisconsin that day.

Our son couldn't handle being in his car seat that long and spent most of the time crying. We only stopped for gas, about every 300 miles, and that's when we would use the bathroom and stretch our legs for a bit.

By the time we hit western Minnesota it was extremely late and I demanded we stop and get a hotel room. Rich refused, saying he wasn't going to waste the money. Adam and I were miserable and were both crying by then. I got so angry and yelled at Rich to stop the damn van at a hotel because we couldn't take it anymore. I told him he could leave us there if he was so hell-bent on getting home in one day. Rich yelled back that he was so sick of my BS that he'd gladly dump me off and he and Adam would go home without me. I fired back saying I'd call the police, because what he was doing—keeping our son stuck in his car seat all day—was a form of child abuse.

Rich must have believed me, because he pulled into the very next hotel and we stayed there for the night. He was highly agitated, so I opted to sleep in the second bed with Adam.

For the remainder of our eight-hour drive home the next day, Rich gave me the silent treatment.

Attempting Therapy

My sister, Angela (not her real name), was pursuing a psychology doctorate. Over the years, she had shared different things she learned in her classes about mental illness. We spoke on numerous occasions about my crazy mother-in-law, Rich's brother who committed suicide, and what growing up in that environment might have been like. As things got progressively worse in my marriage, I began to share more details with Angela. She could tell I was pretending to be happy and encouraged me to try therapy so I could figure out what I wanted for my future.

After that family vacation, I decided to heed my sister's suggestion to see a therapist. Instead of going to work on myself, I went wanting to find out what was wrong with my husband so I could teach him and try to help him change. At the first session I puked out all my background information—my family of origin, my job and education histories, and my husband's background.

The therapist thanked me in an annoyed tone for my life's résumé and then asked what the issue was that brought me to therapy. I told her how my husband had behaved on our trip and how I wanted him to change but he wouldn't. I was crying and going on and on. She held up her hand to stop me and bluntly said, "Jodi, you need to stop right now. I hear you about your husband and how he won't change. Are you trying to ask me what I think you should do?" I nodded yes. She said, "Jodi, you need to shit or get off the pot. Either you decide to divorce him or you suck it up and stay."

Oh my God, what a total bitch! Who did she think she was? How dare she tell me to get divorced?! That wasn't my goal! I didn't get married and have a baby to end up divorced. I was angry and freaked out by how she spoke to me and I never went back.

That experience threw me into a state of deep denial. I refused to consider what the therapist had said and convinced myself that my marriage wasn't that bad. I furthered my efforts of trying to teach, fix, and change my husband.

Dream Home Heartbreak

Rich and I worked in the city and commuted separately 45 minutes to work each day. We staggered our schedules so Adam wasn't with the babysitter too long. The commute was expensive and all of our work friends who lived closer encouraged us to move to be nearer to our work.

Rich and I had talked about the idea and even gone to some open houses, but Rich always found issues with them. Much to my surprise, however, he agreed that we could buy a parcel of land outside the city, with the intention of building. He was all in on the idea.

The house plans were drawn up—it was going to be our dream house. When it was time to go to the bank and start the construction loan, Rich said he wasn't going to saddle himself with a big mortgage payment. It didn't matter that we were pre-approved and could afford the monthly payments—he wasn't going to have anything to do with it. I was devastated and withdrew from him, focusing my attention on anything else possible to get my mind off of the heartbreak. Over the next few months I barely spoke to him.

That winter, a house in the small town where we lived went on the market and, much to my surprise, Rich said we should buy it. I quickly jumped at the idea—anything to get us out of the dinky little house we'd been renting for the past five years.

We bought the house and then we were both on a high over owning our first home. I put all of my energy into decorating plans. There were lots of updates the house needed but we didn't have enough money without taking out a home equity loan, so I agreed we could sell our parcel of land. Once that sold, we were able to do work on our house to replace the roof, windows, doors, paint the house, add a deck, landscape the yard, and finish half of the basement into additional living space.

When our focus was on the house projects our relationship seemed better.

Feeling Restless

As I continued through my bachelor's program, I began to feel restless with the job I'd had for the last four years. I was still in the middle of my degree program so I didn't fit the requirements to apply for the job advancements I wanted. I was met with opposition when I talked with Rich about the idea of leaving my job. He said he wasn't going to be the sole provider for the family and that I had to work to help pay half the bills. Within a few months, I found a full-time job only 15 minutes from home that paid more.

My new job was going pretty well, as was school, and I was beginning to see the end in sight. At the same time, Rich was beginning to get bored with his job and decided to take classes to become a first responder and emergency medical technician (EMT). We balanced our work and school schedules pretty well, and it was honestly nice to have him away for a few hours every week so I could have some down time for myself after Adam went to bed.

We both loved Halloween and decided to go to the opening night of Fright Fest at Six Flags Great America, near Chicago. We had a blast! A month later, I found out I was pregnant. Only a week later, I miscarried. I had never experienced a miscarriage before and was very upset—it felt like such a loss. Rich never tried to console me. The evening of the miscarriage, as I was crying in bed he told me—in a cold, annoyed tone—that I had to get over it. I felt so alone.

The environment at my job had declined swiftly in the weeks prior to my miscarriage to the point that it was time to find a new job, fast. Rich said the issues at work were only in my head, but I knew he was wrong. I found a marketing job at a bank in another town only 20 minutes from home. I went from full-time to 32 hours a week, but by then Rich was working part-time as an EMT and was able to make up the drop in our household income by picking up extra shifts on the weekend, which he didn't mind.

The Baby Itch Returns

I knew I wanted another baby and thought it might make things better. I heard from friends and coworkers that a second child had really helped to ground their husbands. I foolishly assumed another child would force Rich to be more involved and, hopefully, finally change into the emotionally stable and loving man I had always dreamed about.

We had our second son, William (not his real name), in October of 1998. Big brother, Adam, who was three-and-a-half by then, was so excited to have a baby brother to play with.

Much to Rich's displeasure, I took twelve weeks of unpaid maternity leave. I kept Adam home with me to save on sitter costs.

William was a happy and hungry baby, wanting to eat every couple of hours, around the clock. I was exhausted from lack of sleep, trying to spend time with Adam, and getting no help from Rich. He said if I was taking three months off work, then I would have to continue to take care of both kids, and that included keeping up with everything else around the house. When I didn't keep up, he'd complain that I was being lazy. But that time, instead of jumping into action when he barked, I would leave things as they were and say assertively, "Sorry, but I'm exhausted and I'd appreciate if you'd help me out for a change." He rarely did.

I couldn't shake the surreal experience I had after William was born, when I understood that the second baby wasn't going to change things. I also found that I had more self-confidence and wasn't afraid to stand up to Rich. That was a big change in my behavior. With the responsibilities of having two kids, Rich was more easily agitated. If Adam accidentally spilled his milk at the table or broke a toy, Rich yelled at him and made him cry. Anytime that happened, I'd jump in to protect my boys and call Rich out on his behavior. That shifted his yelling away from the boys to me instead. Afterward, he'd go sulk in another room for the rest of the night.

It truly felt like we were "walking on eggshells" around Rich, and I was beginning to really worry about the boys' well-being and how Rich's behavior could affect them as they got older. I was thinking more about what that assertive therapist had said and was beginning to think she might have been right—I needed to suck it up or leave.

Marriage Counseling

Rich's reactive anger outbursts were increasing to the point where it was becoming too much for me to manage. I tried to talk to him about his behavior, but he always found a way to spin it around and blame me for not doing enough around the house, being selfish, or neglecting the kids. His accusations were very hurtful. I was always caring for the kids and managing the household chores, in addition to working, and I rarely got the chance to relax. Even if I was sick, he still wouldn't help.

Although I was less scared than I had been before about the idea of getting divorced, I was far from ready. In my mind, I still had hope and thought marriage counseling might help.

When I brought up the idea of marriage counseling, Rich refused. The more I tried to persuade him to agree, the harder he dug his heels in. I was so frustrated with him and his resistance that, in response to an argument on that topic, I stopped speaking to him. That went on for a couple of weeks. It felt very empowering and initially was quite peaceful.

At first, he acted like he didn't care, then he got angry with me. The longer I continued being silent, the more he tried to woo me back. When Rich finally caved and agreed to go to marriage counseling, I was flooded with a sense of hope that he was willing to take responsibility and change his behavior.

I was excited for the appointment (with a different therapist than the one I'd been to before), but when I met Rich in the waiting room, he was very agitated. During the session, he pointed out my flaws and blamed me for our marital problems, saying I created issues when there were none, and that I was selfish and neglected the kids. I was speechless and wanted to walk out, but I stayed because I didn't want to be rude.

I sat there listening to all of his BS, and when it was my turn to speak, I brought up Rich's awful childhood, the big issues he'd had to deal with growing up, and my concern over that being the root cause of our marital issues. Much to my surprise, the therapist revealed that his approach was not to look back and dissect the past, but rather look at today's issues and have us work on making changes from where we were. The look of hatred Rich shot me at that moment revealed clearly that he considered that my payback, and that he had won.

We never returned for a second session and I dropped any notion or hope of trying to change him. I had been wrong for thinking I could or that it was my job.

A few weeks after returning to work post-maternity leave, I scheduled a free consultation with a divorce attorney. She told me about the "best-case scenarios" and stressed that if couples could agree on splitting assets, debts, and time with the kids, the divorce would be cheaper and faster.

That visit helped to shift my thinking to "It's time to start figuring things out."

Chapter 2

How I Figured It Out

Stress-Related Health Problems

My body started to show signs that I was under extreme stress. After my second son was born, I forgot to eat or had bouts of diarrhea and would easily drop ten pounds in two weeks. I began having breakouts of painful water blisters on the palms of my hands. Then, at a routine dental checkup, the dentist felt a growth in my neck and referred me to my family physician to have it checked. An ultrasound revealed that I had an enlarged thyroid, but they never found any medical issues and attributed it to stress.

The loudest signal my body sent was panic attacks. The first one was the most frightening. I saw my family doctor a few hours afterward and they ran a CAT scan but couldn't find anything medically wrong.

The doctor said that panic attacks can often be brought on by high amounts of stress. When she asked if I was feeling stressed, I said yes and looked out of the corner of my eye toward Rich, who was sitting next to me. She picked up on my hint right away. I quickly said that it was hard juggling everything—taking care of both boys, working, and managing the household chores. She kindly suggested I consider talking to a therapist to get help with managing my stress. She emphasized to Rich that it was very important that I follow through and that he help make sure I was able to go. He willingly agreed.

This was the golden ticket that allowed me to return to individual therapy without opposition, as Rich never argued with a doctor's diagnosis or suggestions.

The Truth Revealed

Figuring things out included finally working on me. I returned to individual therapy, but this time did some advance research. I picked a therapist named Kathy (not her real name). She was very sweet and I felt safe speaking with her.

I was a bit hesitant to discuss my marriage, because I didn't want to slide backward into trying to fix Rich, so I kept that out of the forefront of the conversation as much as I could. I had always been drawn to personal development and focused my learning on broadening my perspective and how to parent more effectively and be a good role model for my kids.

I busted my ass reading and attending seminars, and felt really good about how much I learned within a few months. At one point, I caught myself sharing some of my exciting new insights with Rich, but he thought it was brainwashing and a waste of time. I ignored him and simply stopped sharing.

The day after a big argument with Rich, I had a session with Kathy. When I walked into her office, she could tell something was wrong. I shared what had happened, how upset I was, and my concern for my boys' well-being. Looking back, I think she already knew by then that my marriage was messed up, but was waiting for the right time to dig deeper. That was the day.

We talked for a while about Rich and about our relationship. Then Kathy pulled out a piece of paper and handed it to me. It had a big circle and a couple of inner circles, and lots of words printed all over it. She asked me to circle all the words that described my relationship with my husband and told me that there were no right or wrong answers. "Circle anything that fits with what it's been like," she said.

I looked at the list and feverishly began circling and circling. When I finished, she said, "Okay, now I want you to turn it over and circle all the words on the other side of the paper that describe and match your relationship." There were dozens of words, as many as on the other side, but they were different. They were all positive. I struggled to circle even two words on the new side of the paper.

When I asked her what it was about, she told me, "The side where you only circled two words represents a healthy relationship." Then she turned the paper back over and said, "This side represents an unhealthy and abusive relationship."

I felt numb as I stared at the paper, flipping it over and over again. Only two words on the healthy relationship side. My heart sank.

I looked up at her and said, "My sister told me years ago that she thinks Rich has a personality disorder, but I never really read much into it. He's always said everything is my fault and that I make him behave the way he does." Kathy looked at me, leaned in, and very seriously said, "Jodi, you're not crazy and this is not your fault. What your sister shared with you could very well be true, but it's not your job to diagnose him or fix him. Or teach him how to be a better husband or dad. He has to want to do that for himself."

I sobbed as it all sank in deeper. Kathy encouraged me to give myself time to let it settle in and suggested I not share my new insights with Rich, as she feared it might possibly cause backlash. I agreed to keep it to myself.

From that point on, I started reading and researching about emotional abuse and personality disorders. So much of the information in the many articles and books I read matched what I had been experiencing. Everything was making more sense to me and I felt so relieved, because I wasn't crazy like he'd always said I was. He'd had me believing for so long that I had done something wrong to incite his behaviors and reactions, but in truth I was collateral damage—and so were the boys.

Facing Shame

I thought about all the years I wasted beating myself up trying to fix, teach, and change Rich into the man I thought he was capable of being. But after that therapy session with Kathy, when I looked at him, it was with different eyes. The potential I thought I'd seen in him wasn't him—it was actually me and my potential. I was trying to mirror that to him, but I had to realize that wasn't how it worked. He wasn't willing to change.

I felt deep shame that I'd brought two children into the world and tried to build a family that was destined to implode. And that I'd exposed my children to emotional abuse when I should have been protecting them better. I felt bad about the emotional damage they had each endured so far, and how it might continue to negatively affect them in years to come. My oldest son was already displaying disrespectful behavior toward me and was having more meltdowns at home and school when he felt any level of stress.

I was also worried that I'd be harshly judged by my family. There was a level of "life success" attached to getting married, having a family, and reaching milestone anniversaries. I had invested nearly half of my life with Rich, and now was thinking of breaking up our family.

I knew my parents would take it the hardest and I didn't want to let them down. What I didn't realize was that Rich had been showing glimpses of his real self around my family, but nobody ever called him out on his poor behavior. They just thought he was a big jerk. I learned later that my family was worried about how Rich's behavior was affecting me and the boys.

I felt insecure and worried about what friends and acquaintances would think of me. We lived in a small town where everyone knew each other, and the majority of our friends still lived in the area. We were one of the first in our group to get married and start a family, and now we'd be the first to split up.

All that shame took a back seat to the fact that I knew I needed to do something or else we would be stuck forever in that hell. I knew it was my responsibility to get myself and my boys out and to give my boys a chance at a better life.

Trusting My Intuition

My sister Angela had become involved with a women's support organization called Woman Within. She attended weekend retreats, participated in monthly e-circle groups, and also helped to staff weekend retreats. Woman Within helped women empower themselves so they could pursue their dreams, live their ideal lives, and feel happy. When Angela encouraged me to attend a weekend retreat, I jumped at the opportunity.

That was a transformative experience for me. The first night, they took us through a deep descent meditation, where we visualized walking through the various rooms of a castle.

When I walked into the dining hall of the castle, I saw visions of an unconditionally loving and supportive man who I knew was going to be my future husband. I couldn't see his face, but his actions spoke loudly. He was safe, and wanted to take care of me. I remember crying as I lay there on the floor. I could feel that man as though he were real. That visualization exercise opened me up to feeling hopeful about my future.

The next day, we were broken into smaller groups and each woman shared her individual issue that had brought her to that retreat. Afterward, each woman went through a specific exercise designed to help process and let go of the obstacles that were holding her back from attaining her dreams. The rest of the group witnessed each woman's exercise, as a secondary learning experience.

When it was my turn, I shared that my husband was mean and that I felt trapped in my marriage and didn't know what to do. The group leader asked a few probing questions and talked with me about fear and not trusting my intuition. She gave me the option of three different exercises, two of which had already been done by others. So I picked the third one, which was a trust fall.

I climbed on top of a high counter, stood on the edge and then fell backward (like in the old Nestea plunge commercials) into the laced arms of 20 women. I cried as they cradled me and sang a song. I felt so safe, supported, and loved. That helped me to welcome my intuition back and supported me in letting my intuition guide me going forward.

Acceptance and Forgiveness

The combination of therapy and the transformative experiences at the women's retreat led me deeper into evaluating my entire relationship with Rich, all the way back to when we met. I asked myself questions such as: What was the draw to that type of person? Why hadn't I gotten out earlier when the stakes weren't so high? Where did I get so lost?

My young age and limited life experience were the biggest culprits. I had followed the values taught by my family: helping others in need. I hadn't understood that there were degrees of helping—from being supportive, to caretaking, to the most extreme, codependency. I took the advice of "being there" for Rich too literally and, in doing so, began to lose myself.

It took some time to accept the fact that I was in a dead-end marriage, and to forgive myself for not seeing all the signs and acting on them sooner. I'd gotten to a place where I was better able to trust my intuition, and I knew I and my boys were ultimately going to be okay.

Success Does Not Require Only One Marriage

With my blinders off and my awareness radar on, I was able to finally see, hear, and remember things so much better. I paid attention to other married couples who'd been together various lengths of time, listened to their stories, and was able to identify which couples were happily married and which were not. I also tuned in when people who had been divorced talked about their lives.

What I saw with the miserable couples was that many of them stayed together for the kids. The wife didn't have enough skills or education to find a decent and well-paying job, so she felt she couldn't leave. Or it was cheaper to stay together until the kids reached 18, to avoid anyone having to pay child support.

I also noticed happy divorcees who were creating lives they'd always wanted, as well as couples in happy second marriages. It was so refreshing to see those options. I was finally able to drop the notion that success required having only one marriage.

Fear Not

While I was certain I wanted to get out of my marriage, I had no idea how actually to do it. The divorce attorney I went to for the free consultation talked very generally about the divorce process, but said nothing about how to pre-plan for it. I didn't feel like there was anyone I could really talk to who had been through a divorce and could be a good mentor.

Over the years, during extreme arguments, when I hinted to Rich that maybe we should split up because it wasn't working, he made statements that he would never pay for a house he wasn't living in, that I'd never be able to make it on my own, and that he'd never let me have the kids or any of his stuff. I believed him.

I also knew that if I stayed I'd die a slow and painful death, and my kids would turn into disrespectful jerks. I envisioned what my boys might be like five and ten years in the future if we stayed... and that vision was horrible. I saw them behaving like their dad—blaming everyone else and not being accountable, being quick to anger, having explosive outbursts, and manipulating others to get what they wanted. I also knew they'd be even more disrespectful than they already were toward me and other women. I didn't want them to repeat the cycles they were being exposed to. The benefits of leaving my husband outweighed the risks.

Ready, Fire, Aim

I had continued with therapy and researching about emotional abuse. My self-esteem was getting stronger by the week. I no longer felt small and insignificant. That enabled me to ignore Rich's narcissistic behavior more often, versus trying to teach him how to behave. Gone were the days of explaining to Rich how his particular behavior hurt my feelings (or the boys') and telling him better ways he could've expressed his opinion or reacted. When he yelled at the kids, I still stepped in to try to shield them, and I wasn't afraid to point out when he was being mean and abusive towards us.

It was the morning of July 5, 2001. The day prior was spent with family and friends celebrating Independence Day at our house. I was in a different frame of mind and was ready to sit Rich down and tell him I wanted out of the marriage. My thought was that, despite how he had treated me over the years, talking with him in a calm, respectful manner would be best. I wasn't exactly sure how he'd react, but I was hopeful he'd see that we were both miserable and that this would be the best option.

Rich and I went out on the patio to talk. The conversation lasted only a few minutes. I explained how I felt about our marriage and that I thought we should separate. He said nothing and got up and walked into the house. I felt a huge sense of relief and assumed we'd probably talk more later about how we were going to handle things. When I walked into the house, Rich was pulling out all of the beer and wine coolers from the refrigerator that had been left over from the party we'd had the day before. He proceeded to guzzle down bottle after bottle. I asked him what he was doing and he said, "Well, seeing as you don't want to be married to me anymore, I may as well drink." I walked away, thinking that if I ignored him he'd knock it off. I went to get the kids dressed for the day.

I kept to myself most of the day, doing household chores and keeping an eye on the kids while they played. In the afternoon, I noticed that Rich was outside cleaning the lawn tractor. The boys had gone out to play in the yard and watch their dad.

Before that point, the boys didn't know anything about our morning conversation. A few minutes later, I saw Adam sitting on the lawn tractor and I could hear him crying. I went out to see what had happened only to hear Adam yelling that he hated me for wanting to leave Dad and wreck our family, and that he wanted to live with his dad. My heart sank.

When I looked at Rich, I could see the anger and smugness in his eyes. In that instant, I knew he was trying to use the boys as pawns and to punish me. I had foolishly given Rich the benefit of the doubt, thinking that my calm and respectful approach would lead him to be mature and reasonable. I was dead wrong.

I made the kids go inside and I asked Rich what that stunt was all about. He replied in a pissed-off tone, saying, "Nothing I did for you was ever good enough, and I'm so sick of you treating us like shit." He got in his vehicle and drove away. I had no idea where he was going, and I honestly didn't care. I was able to settle the boys down. I tried to ease their worries about what had happened and explain things.

Later that evening, after the boys had been in bed a few hours, I received a call from the owner of the local sports bar saying that my husband was there and that he was in no condition to drive. I called my parents, who lived nearby, and asked if they could come over to stay at the house while I went to get Rich from the bar.

As soon as my dad arrived, I left. When I got to the bar, Rich was a total mess. It was apparent that he had been crying, and he could barely sit on the barstool anymore. The bartender said, "I cut him off a while ago and told him to call for a ride, but he wouldn't. He also said you want to get divorced." I thanked the bartender for calling me and I talked Rich into coming home with me so he could sleep it off. I said we'd talk more about things the next day.

On the short drive home, he sobbed and pleaded saying, "Jodi, I can't do this like you can. It's not easy for me." I looked at him and very confidently said, "Well, you're gonna have to figure it out because we're not living like this anymore. I'm done."

When we arrived home, I told Rich my dad was in the house. Rich freaked out and stormed into the house, yelling at my dad, saying he was trespassing and had to leave. Rich threatened to beat up my dad if he didn't go. My dad is not a confrontational person and tried to explain that he had come over to stay at the house with the boys while I was gone.

Rich grabbed his phone and called 911, demanding that the police come. My dad and I were both shocked by his irrational behavior. My dad wanted to go, but didn't want to leave me alone. I decided to call the police as well, and told them my husband was extremely intoxicated and had threatened my dad.

Within minutes, there were two sheriffs at our house. They spoke separately to Rich and my dad, and then one of the officers came inside to speak to me. I was very upset, and embarrassed that Rich's behavior had gotten so out of hand. Because he didn't physically touch me or my dad, the sheriffs couldn't arrest him. But they did tell Rich that he couldn't stay at home and had to go sleep it off somewhere else. He called a childhood friend and stayed at his house for the night. I felt relieved Rich was gone. The boys had slept through the ruckus and had no idea what had happened.

The next morning, I told the boys that their dad had been paged on an early ambulance call. I still felt embarrassed by what had happened, but I knew for sure I didn't want to be married to Rich anymore.

Later that afternoon, Rich called to talk with me. He apologized for how he'd behaved, said he'd been way out of line, and blamed the majority of his stress on his job. He told me how much he loved me and our boys, and that our family was the most important thing to him. Then he said he wanted to change, didn't want to get divorced, and begged me to let him come home. He sounded so different than he ever had before. He sounded sincere and respectful and loving towards me—that was uncharted territory. I told him I'd have to think about it and would call him back.

Shortly after that, I called my parents to give them an update. When I told them how Rich spoke to me on the call I'd just had with him, they immediately blamed his behavior the night before on all the alcohol he'd drunk. They said that it sounded like he was willing to fix things. I tried to explain my side, but my mom said the whole ordeal was embarrassing, getting divorced would be too devastating on the kids, and maybe Rich could just go to counseling.

Even in this situation, divorce was not an option in my parents' eyes. I felt torn. I loved my parents, but wasn't sold on the way they looked at things. I felt they weren't really taking my feelings into consideration, which hurt. When I tried to talk further with them about how I felt, they got frustrated with me. I was back to the place of feeling unsure about what to do. A few hours later, I called Rich and told him he could come home.

In the months that followed, Rich seemed so different. He was happy all the time and behaved decently toward me and the kids. He also did not drink. If he started feeling frustrated, he wouldn't take it out on us, but would go into another room to calm down. He began working even more EMT shifts, on top of his full-time job working with computers, but still made an effort to spend time with the boys and help me around the house. It was quite strange for me to see him behave like this. My intuition still told me to stay alert, which I did.

A few weeks later, Rich bought me an expensive diamond anniversary band. It was beautiful, but I still wasn't convinced he had changed. My parents saw his gesture as a true sign that he was trying. I ignored their opinion and remained suspicious.

Gearing Up

With the completion of my bachelor's degree, I was able to secure a part-time, grant-funded job that allowed me to work from home. I set a work schedule and was adamant that the kids still went to daycare during the day—Adam after school and William all day. The time home alone each day allowed me to start laying out my exit plan. To get out of the house a few nights a week and earn some extra money, I also became a direct-sales consultant doing parties in other people's homes. I had to open a separate bank account and credit card, per our tax accountant's recommendation, and quietly tucked all my profits away into a separate savings account that Rich had no access to.

I felt good about my progress toward leaving Rich, and put a number of other changes in motion—like purging and selling household and baby items we no longer needed, and organizing our stuff—but I still wasn't exactly sure how to go about the actual leaving. I didn't see how I could safely leave with the boys without it triggering the same reaction and craziness as before.

I also didn't want to make any mistakes along the way as I kept planning that would tip Rich off that I was still wanting to leave the marriage. So I pretended I was happy that we were still together and carried on with the day-to-day stuff, to ward off any suspicions.

My work-from-home position ended unexpectedly due to the company's budget cuts, so I had to find a new position. I was fortunate to get a full-time job outside of the house doing marketing work for the business program at a community college in the city. One of my fellow coworkers, Bruce, taught program classes and also happened to be a former family law attorney. We struck up a friendship and spoke frequently about the projects his classes were working on, current events, and even some of the experiences he'd had with his former clients. I mentally tagged him as a resource to bounce things off of sometime.

That sometime ended up coming a lot sooner than I'd anticipated.

The Last Straw

Rich slowly reverted back to his old self—easily angered, snapping at the boys, putting me down, and complaining all the time that I wasn't doing enough around the house, or complaining about his full-time job. I returned to shielding the boys from his behavior and standing up for myself when he took his frustrations out on me.

It was April 2002, and my youngest sister, Marie (not her real name), was getting married. The ceremony and reception were being held in the city, so we had made reservations for the four of us to stay at the hotel next door to the banquet hall.

On the way to the wedding ceremony, Rich told me he was sick of working in the computer field and was going to quit his job and only work as a part-time EMT. I was furious at this ridiculous idea and, with my maturing self-respect, told him absolutely not. We had a mortgage, he'd just gotten a new truck that came with a hefty payment, and with all of our other bills there was no way I was going to be able to support all of us if he cut back on work. I reminded him of our agreement that his EMT wages would go toward his monthly truck payment.

He tried to argue further about it, but I said "No." He called me a selfish bitch when I refused to discuss it any further. I had been through so many arguments and had been called so many names over the years that it no longer surprised me. I had become more immune to it.

My non-support triggered his foul mood for the rest of that day. He refused to help watch the boys before the ceremony so that I could pin flowers on the groomsmen and family members. Instead, he chatted and laughed with some of the wedding guests. After the ceremony, the immediate family was requested for pictures, but Rich didn't want to participate. It took my dad to coax him to join us. During dinner, Rich sulked and wouldn't talk to anyone. He snapped at the boys when they didn't sit still or wanted to run around the dance floor during the reception. I tried my best to ignore his behavior and focus on enjoying my sister's special day.

Later in the evening, the boys were getting tired and it was time to take them back to the hotel. Rich refused to do it alone, even though he knew I wanted to stay with my newly married sister. So I went along, with the understanding that I was going to return to the reception and spend more time with my siblings and the guests. Back at the hotel, he threw a fit that I was going back to the reception. I told him I'd only be gone for a short time.

I got the boys ready for bed, gave them kisses, and walked out of the room. Back at the reception, I was able to finally have fun. It was so refreshing not to have him there. A couple of my siblings even commented that I was so much more relaxed when Rich wasn't around. They were right—I really felt that way. When the reception ended at midnight, a small group of us decided to go to a bar a couple of blocks away that had a DJ. We danced and had lots of fun.

When I got back to the hotel, Rich wouldn't let me into our room. My eldest sister, Anne (not her real name), heard me out in the hallway and came out of her room to tell me Rich was really pissed that I had been gone so long. He had demanded that Anne come to our room at shortly after midnight to stay with the boys. She said he was steaming mad when he got back without me. Apparently, he'd gone to find me when we were already at the bar dancing.

My other sister, Angela, who had been with me at the bar, pounded on the door and told Rich to let me in and to stop being such a jerk and that I hadn't done anything wrong. He finally opened the door and let me in. My sisters went back to their rooms down the hall.

The look on Rich's face scared the hell out of me. His eyes were filled with rage and hatred. He got right in my face and yelled at me and called me names.

Every ounce of strength I'd had instantly vanished. I felt defeated. When I attempted to go to the bed to lie down, he stood in my way and said I could sleep on the floor. I was sobbing and terrified. The boys were wide-awake and both crying too. I had not seen this degree of rage from Rich before. Both boys ran over and clung to me, and I could tell they were terrified. I wanted to run out of the room, but I knew Rich would never let me take the boys, I couldn't get them out on my own, and there was no way I was going to leave them. I ended up crawling in bed with my boys, but I barely slept all night. I knew it was time to ask for help so we could get out safely.

The next morning, Rich got the boys dressed and was playing with them. He told me to go take a shower and then we'd all go down to eat brunch with my family. When we were around my family, he acted like nothing had happened, but when we were alone I got the silent treatment.

It's Go Time

The following Monday at work I asked Bruce if we could speak privately. He could tell something was wrong by my demeanor. I told him I really needed his help. I gave him the run-down of what had happened over the weekend, and about the craziness I had dealt with over our relationship, from dating to the present. I told Bruce I wanted to leave Rich and had been slowly planning things, because I knew he wouldn't voluntarily let us leave, but that in light of Rich's recent behavior, I needed to get the hell out of my marriage as soon as possible.

Bruce was very supportive. He said, "I agree. You need to leave him. He's very unstable and it's in your and your boys' best interest to get out of that hostile environment. You have the choice to leave right away and try to fight for things—personal items and money—but you'll probably get screwed. Or you can plan a smart exit strategy. I'm more than happy to walk you through how to do it so that you come out of it financially whole and, hopefully, retain primary placement of your kids."

I was so appreciative of Bruce's help and listened intently as he shared what he knew from his years as a divorce attorney. He renewed my hope in being able to get out safely and swiftly, and filled in the blanks of the steps that had been missing from my plan.

I got started right away because time was of the essence. I needed to be free!

Chapter 3
The Road To Freedom

The road to freedom begins with the end in mind. Take a moment to envision where you ideally want to be and what you want your life to look like. Let yourself go there, to that place in your mind where life feels hopeful and looks beautiful. Imagine a life where you feel free, where you can be yourself completely, free of the drama, chaos, and stress. Free to discover (or rediscover) who you are. Free to be happy and do the things you enjoy and want to do. And free to raise and nurture your kids in a healthy and loving atmosphere. My dear, you can have all of that! Your wishes and dreams can become reality—your new normal—but only if you believe that you deserve it.

As you've seen from my story, it was pretty easy for me to get sucked into the abuse cycle. Yes, I was young and naïve, and easily influenced by my family and the cultural environment at the time. But even as

I stumbled along through that entire relationship I knew deep within myself that I did deserve better—much, much better!

Gains, Not Losses

There's nothing wrong with you wanting to get the hell out of your toxic marriage. It's your legal and personal right. You don't have to stay in a marriage where you feel like you are always put last or that you must consistently care-take and cater to your spouse. And you especially do *not* have to put up with being verbally and emotionally abused.

It's completely healthy to drop the notion that being married—even to a jerk—is better than being alone. I assure you, it's not. You're gaining by dropping the thoughts that being married is the only way to *be happy*, that putting up with your husband's poor behavior is something you're "supposed to do," and that "no marriage is perfect." I get that no marriage is perfect, but who really, truly wants to put up with ten, 20, 30 or more years with an abusive jerk where you continue to put your life and happiness on hold? I sure didn't and I hope you don't either.

This is an opportunity, because you'll be able to figure out how to stand on your own. And what's ironic is when you're in a relationship that's emotionally abusive and there are kids involved, you're *already* single parenting. You're taking care of so much, and you know how to do most of it because you've been expected to do it all. So while it might seem scary as hell to let go of that other person, you already know you can do it, that you can take care of everything. If you're expected to work full-time and take care of the kids full-time and the house and the bills, whatever it is—you already know how to do it. So when you're on your own it's not going to be much different. Actually, it'll be better, because you won't have your husband's BS in the way.

Leaving your unhealthy marriage is not losing, it's gaining—it's an expansion of your life, of your opportunities and your potential. It's an investment in your future—yours and your kids'. It's saving your life so that you can have the life you truly want and deserve. You have choices and don't need to settle for being treated like garbage.

Wanting to leave, wanting to free yourself, is not selfish, it's *selfless*, especially when you're trying to save yourself and your kids from emotional abuse. Leaving your marriage is you finally taking care of yourself. In doing so, you're making space for your future ex-husband to grow up, to stand on his own, and figure it out. You're giving him the opportunity to move on with his life.

A Bit About Divorce

There are those who struggle with the idea of divorce. Maybe because of their religious or cultural beliefs, how they were raised, or just personal preference. Divorce can have a very negative stigma attached to it that's laced with judgment and shame, especially when there are kids involved, and even if there's abuse present. It's easy to judge others, and doing so almost seems to be human nature. I'm sure there were times when you were quick to judge others, and times when you felt harshly judged. Judgments can sting, but it's the shame that can have a lasting impact and keep you stuck in an unhealthy and unsafe situation.

I have a secret to share that the anti-divorce folks don't know: Getting divorced is one of *the* most empowering and freeing experiences you will ever have. It's a life-changer for the better. You can finally breathe and feel at peace. You'll have the opportunity to explore life for yourself, and to be able to feel whole all on your own. You don't need a spouse to make you feel complete. A spouse, or any relationship for that matter, should be like an accessory—you're here to benefit each other, not be a punching bag or slave to an abusive jerk.

You will enjoy the simple pleasures of life—like watching a TV show or movie of your choice, reading a book or magazine for pleasure, going for a walk or taking your time shopping, and even just cuddling with your kids—free of stress. You won't have to worry about anyone holding you back from doing anything you want to do.

Divorce opened up so many opportunities for me. I met new people and created a brand-new life for myself and my kids. I moved to the suburbs outside the city where I worked. My kids were able to attend a better school and made friends quickly. I traded in my minivan and bought a new car—the exact one I'd wanted.

Eighteen months after my divorce I bought my own home, which felt so frigging awesome. Five years later, I returned to school, earned a master's degree, and changed careers from working in corporate America to teaching communications and business classes at a local college. None of that would have been possible had I stayed in my abusive marriage.

Understanding Abuse

It's not only the young and naïve who are at risk of falling prey to someone with borderline or narcissistic personality disorder. Becoming a victim can happen to anyone, anywhere, regardless of demographics and socioeconomic status. Then chaos becomes the norm. For many emotional abuse victims, it can feel like walking through a mine field—not knowing where to step next to avoid triggering the abuser's nasty behavior. That uncertainty creates stress that breeds second-guessing your decisions, all of which pulls you far away from following your intuition.

Emotional abusers live in a chaotic state in their minds and are usually very insecure due to being victims of childhood abuse themselves (abuse that they never processed or healed from), or because they have a more severe mental illness. They are emotionally dependent on you, their muse, and will take any measures necessary to keep you in line, including constant criticism, shaming, manipulation, bullying, intimidation, as well as threats. The depth and breadth of their actions can vary. They behave differently at home than when around others and can easily switch between their Dr. Jekyll and Mr. Hyde personas.

Regardless of the abuser's background or mental health status, the reason they are the way they are is *not* your responsibility. Some will act like martyrs and use their backgrounds as a hook for your empathy. They tend to thrive on being with people who have big hearts and want to help people, or who are young and naïve. Above all, the abuser's behaviors and the fact that they are abusive are *not* your fault. Nor is it your fault that this happened to you. There were many days when the only way to push those bad thoughts out of my head was to repeat aloud to myself when I was alone, "Jodi, it's not your fault. This is not your fault. You're going to get out of this and be okay."

People on the outside who've never experienced emotional abuse or witnessed it first-hand cannot fully understand what it's like and may even say (or think) you're making it up or blowing things out of proportion. Or they may get angry at you for allowing yourself to stay in a bad situation for so long. Again, unless they've lived it, they cannot comprehend the mind-control and intimidation that happens.

The Freedom Framework™

What I learned by leaving my abusive marriage and taking the steps to break free isn't for the weak-hearted, but it was absolutely worth it. I had to step into my power, fully embrace it, and work hard. I had a responsibility to myself as an intelligent woman and as a mother to protect my kids. I was willing to take the necessary steps and potential risks to give us a better future. And that's exactly what I want for you—a better future.

I've pooled all of my experience and trial-and-error efforts, research, interviews with emotional abuse survivors, my clients' experiences, as well as insight from legal professionals into a process I call The FREEDOM Framework™. It's what I wished I would have had years ago to help guide me through the process of leaving my marriage, so it would've been easier and wouldn't have taken so long.

The following chapters walk you through each of the seven steps of The FREEDOM Framework™, including to-dos and how-to's, what to avoid, and why these steps are important. Based on your personal situation, you can select the things to do that work best for you.

The FREEDOM Framework™ is an easy-to-follow guide intended to educate you on what you can do in preparation for leaving your marriage and what to expect after you leave. It can help you better prepare, based on your personal situation, and also help you keep your wits about you while you're going through this emotional and physical disconnection process. Some of the chapters contain a lot of information and important reminders to help you stay on track. But not to worry, you can download a handy checklist to help you through the action steps in the various chapters by going to www.ijustwantoutbook.com.

Plus, I will be right here in this book walking alongside you throughout your journey to freedom. You can trust that this process will help you reach your goal of leaving your marriage. And it can help you open up space so you can create the life you've always dreamed about—for yourself and your kids. It also offers the opportunity for you to teach your kids, by example, about self-respect and healthy relationship boundaries.

Freedom Framework™ Steps

F = Free Your Mind…And the Rest Will Follow—The first step in The FREEDOM Framework™ process discusses thoughts versus emotions, what's holding you back, assigning new labels, stepping into character, and being patient.

R = Research and Documentation—The second step will go into detail about the data-gathering process—what to look for and why. It's crucial to know the full business side of your marriage. We'll also look at the benefits of technology and its various uses.

E = Evaluate Your Current Situation—Step three is the check-in phase—where are you and what's the right pace. You'll learn how to build your support network, what various things to consider, and how to manage everything.

E = Exercise Your Rights—The next step in the FREEDOM Framework™ will look at your financials and discuss setting up separate accounts, safe storage options, retirement fund options, and researching and interviewing attorneys.

D = Design Your Exit—All the previous steps will allow you to create the exit plan that best fits your situation. We'll touch upon staying on course, continuing to get support from trusted loved ones, looking for a new place to live and potential school/daycare changes for your kids, deciding what you'll need, letting go of attachments, and how to protect yourself.

O = Prepare for Opposition—It's important that you're prepared for potential opposition. Not everyone is going to be supportive of your choice to leave the marriage. This step will prepare you for the potential fallout and distortion campaign, and offers options to consider for talking to your children, divorce statistics, and tips for going head-to-head with fear.

M = Make Your Move—The final step in the FREEDOM Framework™ process is moving day. You'll learn what you'll need to do, what final details to take care of, saying goodbye, letting the cat out of the bag with your spouse, setting up your new home, and additional safety tips.

What to Expect Along Your Journey to Freedom

As you read through the following chapters you may have bouts of fear or self-doubt. You will be learning new concepts and methods, things you may have never considered. Some of the information in the upcoming chapters may even scare the hell out of you. Please be kind to yourself and remember that embarking on a new beginning and rewriting your future can feel nerve-wracking. This is completely normal!

I invite you to take some time to first evaluate where you are now and whether you're ready to step forward. Take those moments to envision the life you want, so you'll have that touchstone, your reason for going through the *FREEDOM Framework*™ process. Then go ahead and read the remainder of this book. When you're done, check back in with yourself to see how you feel. When you're ready to get started, consider this book in helping you create a new and better life for you and your kids.

Chapter 4

Step 1: Free Your Mind…
And The Rest Will Follow

Thoughts Vs. Emotions

The first step in the FREEDOM Framework™ is freeing your mind so that you can continue to move forward and reach your end goal. Freeing your mind does not just happen once and then you're set; rather, it requires continuous attention and focus on your thoughts. Some people believe their emotions drive their thoughts, but our thoughts actually drive our emotions.

To be more specific, it all starts with our circumstances. The circumstances we encounter drive our thoughts, which, in turn, trigger our emotions. Let's say you've just had a nasty argument with your spouse (circumstance), you may wish he would become violently ill or die (thoughts), which can trigger feelings of anger and maybe even guilt later (emotions). The brain works so quickly that the thought and emotion almost seem to happen simultaneously, which is why people assume emotions come before thinking.

Another way to think about attention and focus is like you're stepping outside of your body and observing. For example, if you've ever sat in the food court at the local mall I'm sure you've found yourself people-watching. You're observing the people walking by. Now, let's say you notice a couple sitting nearby who appear to be having an argument. As you focus your attention on that couple you can hear what's being said and you're able to drown out all the other background noise in the mall. You listen intently but you have no vested interest in these people or their situation. *That's* how I want you to pay attention to your thoughts. Tune in, notice what thoughts are going through your mind, but don't get attached to them.

What's Holding You Back

The biggest thing that tends to hold you back is *you*, by simply getting in your own way. Ways to get in your own way include putting things off and hiding behind excuses, such as the many competing priorities in life—kids, schedules, work, lack of time, and even money. Waiting for everything in your life to line up and be perfect will only keep you stuck right where you are.

You might be holding yourself back because you cannot imagine your life without all the drama. Even though you hate it, you've become conditioned to it; therefore, that's your normal. You know what to expect despite how stressful it is, but it's familiar and there's a comfort to that.

Fear of the unknown and, in this case, not knowing exactly what your life might look like on the other side—the escapee side—can also hold you back from leaving. If we were in a coaching session together, this is where I'd remind you to think back to the previous chapter, "The Road to Freedom," and start with the end in mind. Envisioning your goals on a regular basis will help you stay the course.

Another obstacle is if you've allowed yourself to get spooked by horror stories you've heard, and freeze. Stories like, so-and-so's failed attempt to leave her marriage left her with nothing. Or, it was traumatic for the kids so she went back and decided to put up with him until they were out of the house. Honestly, the only reason to listen to the horror stories is to hear them for what they are: learning opportunities. If you were to ask what really happened, they'd probably say it's because she made some big errors or knee-jerk reacted. Learning the details and what she wished had been done differently are key things to note so you can avoid making those same mistakes.

Assigning New Labels

When I shared my story in the earlier chapters, you'll remember I referred to my husband by name (which was changed to protect his identity). I was able to do so because I'm so far removed from that time and emotionally disconnected from him. However, for you, my continual reference to him as "your spouse" or "your husband" may unconsciously keep you emotionally connected to him. Therefore, for the remainder of this book, I will be referring to your future ex-husband as your "soon-to-be-ex," or STBX. I invite you to practice saying it to yourself in your mind and even aloud until it no longer sounds weird. I have a hunch giving him a new label will help free your mind more.

Step Into Character

You've heard the phrase, "fake it 'til you make it," right? Well, that's what stepping into character is all about—pretending everything is just fine at home and in interactions with your STBX to the best of your ability. In the *Harry Potter* movies they introduced the invisibility cloak with which Harry and other characters could move around unseen or observe what others were doing. Your pre-work shouldn't be obvious to anyone and is done in a subtle and secret manner. It happens in the background while your life is still happening—when kids are away at daycare, school, or a friend's house; during sports practices or extra-curricular activities; when you are home alone or after everyone's gone to bed, or even during your lunch break. It's doing online research from your mobile device, making phone calls from work, or organizing financial paperwork while you make note of important details. That's how you hide in plain sight and keep things off radar.

For your personal safety, I do encourage you to become a really good actress. If you've ever seen the movie *Sleeping with the Enemy*, starring Julia Roberts, you'll understand that it's about planning a smart exit strategy before you execute it. Now, I'm certainly not suggesting you fake your death or anything like that, but you can look to certain movies, articles, and books to learn how people have been able to successfully deceive their abuser in order to get out safely. And by stepping into character you are better able to feel empowered and disconnect from your former self.

Stepping into character also carries over into your interactions with family, friends, coworkers, and—especially—on social media sites like Facebook, Twitter, Instagram, LinkedIn, and Pinterest. This includes not posting, sharing, or liking anything that reflects your unhappiness or marital stress, even cryptic-type posts when you're feeling angry or frustrated. Because when you least expect it, somebody is going to notice and start asking questions, start gossiping about what they're seeing in your posts, or—worse yet—tip off your STBX.

A rule of thumb: Keep it simple and pretend all is fine in your world. I totally understand that as you get things in order your STBX is going to keep behaving the same, and may drive you crazy, which leads me to the next topic about being patient.

Patience, My Darling!

Freeing your mind also means being patient as you work through the *FREEDOM Framework*™. By not putting pressure on yourself to get everything done quickly, you can free your mind of any unnecessary stress. Plus, rushing the process could tip off your STBX or cause you to make mistakes that could cost you more in the end. I encourage you to take your time so that you don't miss crucial parts along the way. As you read the next chapters I think you'll understand better why taking it slow is beneficial.

Chapter 5

Step 2: Research And Documentation

This step of research and documentation will enable you to become *very* familiar with your household finances and the "business" side of the marriage. This step will also help shift your thinking more so you can continue to emotionally disconnect from your STBX.

Toward the end of this book you will learn about completing a financial disclosure document for your attorney. This is what the court uses to determine how to split the marital assets and debts. Once you leave, your STBX will not willingly give you copies of information or allow you access to paper copies of online accounts. Knowing your assets, investments, and debts in advance of leaving will save you so much hassle later, and it can potentially save you money during the divorce process (more on that later).

Benefits of Technology

When I first started preparing to leave my abusive marriage it was 2001, saving files to a CD was newer technology. USB drives or saving files to "the Cloud" were still many years away. The closest thing we had to a smartphone was a BlackBerry, which was only used by high-level business professionals. And the idea of paying bills online, accessing online accounts, or having statements emailed was not part of mainstream America yet. I was forced to make photocopies and retain original documents, which meant setting up lots of paper files and physically organizing paperwork. With the wonderful evolution of technology, your research and documentation process can be less conspicuous, but is also potentially more challenging.

As you work through this chapter, assess what technology you have available. Create a new secret email account through Gmail or Yahoo. Do you have access to a printer or scanner? If so, you can make copies and save them electronically to a USB drive, a Cloud account, or email them to yourself (ideally to your new secret email account). Another option, if you own a smartphone or tablet, is to simply take pictures of the documents, send them to your secret email, and then delete the pictures from your phone or tablet. If you prefer to use a USB drive, be sure to keep that hidden or use one from work that your STBX wouldn't be suspicious about.

If you have a newer smartphone or tablet it most likely has security features like entering a passcode or fingerprint recognition. I highly encourage you to use the security features on all your devices. If your STBX questions this, simply blame it on work, and say something along the lines of, "There have been rumors someone is going around to people's desks when they're in meetings, messing with their smartphones and writing embarrassing posts on Facebook, and it's been suggested everyone use the security feature on their phones now."

If you are not currently managing the finances and paying the bills, volunteer to take it over. Tell your spouse that you want to get more involved and help get things more organized. It may entail you convincing your STBX that you getting more involved would take a huge burden off his shoulders.

Once you've taken charge of the finances, make a list of all your accounts and bills, listing logins, passwords, and security questions for each. There are free apps and websites where you can save your personal logins and passwords, and these are easily accessible from your smartphone or computer. The perk of online accounts is that you can usually view previous statements in the bill history. But, if you're like me, and still get some paper bills and statements in the mail, don't hesitate to open them up.

Another idea you may wish to present to your STBX is that you want to shift all of the household statements and bills to electronic and online bill pay to help reduce the amount of mail and piles of old bills that have to get shredded. For those items that still come by mail, such as new credit cards or privacy statements, set up paper files for each for later reference.

Financial Assets and Income

It's important to take ample time to really research and monitor all of your financial assets and income. This includes employment income, bank accounts, cash income, as well as any business income (sole proprietor, LLC, partnership, etc.). A great place to start is by locating your income tax files for the past seven years. This should contain most of the financial information you need, but know that assets and income can also be hidden in places you've never considered, which we'll touch upon more throughout this chapter.

Income Taxes—Whether you complete your own taxes or hire an accountant, all the forms and supporting documentation should be together for each filing year. It's not only important to know where that information is, you will need to make copies or create an electronic file for each tax year. Be sure to label everything clearly for quick access. However, if you cannot make copies, be sure to have the documents ready to take with you when you leave.

Bank/Credit Union Accounts—Take an inventory of *all* the money accounts (checking, savings, escrow, Christmas Club, vacation, kids' savings accounts) for your household, and their current balances. This may include banks, credit unions, PayPal accounts, or other electronic payment accounts, such as Stripe or Square. Monitor the balances to stay on top of all available cash.

If you have separate bank accounts and on some you're not listed as joint account holder, encourage your STBX to still include his login and password on the list. This will enable you to potentially access his bank accounts to check current balances. I do not recommend this, but if your STBX is protective of his bank account and you know his login information, simply pay attention to when he accesses his account and try to also login that same day. In doing so, he may not even become suspicious that you viewed his account.

Financial Income—This can be wages paid from an employer, a stipend for contract work, interest or stock dividends, profit sharing, gambling income (sports, casinos, race tracks), commissions for sales jobs, bonuses (annual or spot) or incentive pay, eBay or Craigslist sales, as well as cash jobs. Your income tax returns should indicate employment income for you and your STBX, and there should be printouts of W2s from each employer.

Kids' Bank Accounts and Investment/College Fund Accounts—If you have savings accounts or any college investment accounts for your child(ren), be sure initially that your name is listed on the account.

This will prevent your STBX from liquidating the funds in your child's account. If only your STBX is listed on the account, you will have no access to protecting that money. If you have access to monitoring those accounts, the only thing you can do is monitor the monthly balances and print copies of the monthly statements.

A work-around with kids' savings accounts, if you are not the parent listed, is to simply open another account at the same bank for your child. This will reduce any suspicion that you're banking at another financial institution. And, because everything is electronic now (e-statements), you can easily set up online access to the new accounts.

For dependent investment or college fund accounts, consult your financial advisor to inquire about balances and options they can offer to protect your children's money. If your STBX is the only parent listed on the dependent investment account, he may decide to liquidate the account. If that happens before your divorce is filed (and you file a joint tax return), you may also be held liable for any surrender fees, early withdrawal penalties, tax penalties, as well as having to claim it as income. If that happens, be sure to also consult a tax professional.

Business—In the event your spouse owns a business or is a partner in a business, please consult with an attorney for further assistance as the laws can vary by business classification and by state.

Retirement Funds and Investments

We primarily think of retirement accounts, like an IRA, 401k or 403b, but also note if there are any pension plans, stocks, or savings bonds. Statements are typically mailed or emailed quarterly. Make note of the balances in each account, as that may be a bargaining chip later during divorce process negotiations. It's common to turn off retirement fund contributions once you get separated, but you can do this at any time. The purpose is to limit the amount your STBX may be awarded in the divorce.

Insurance—Life, Auto, Homeowners, Health, and Dental

If you have a life insurance policy beyond what an employer offers—regular, whole life, or term—contact your agent to verify that your policy is still active and check on the death benefit. Some life insurance policies have cash values that can potentially be cashed in or have loans taken against them. Double check that there is no loan against the policy. Second, verify who is listed as primary and secondary beneficiaries. If your STBX is primary, ask if you can change that to your children instead, or if that's not possible see if you can add your children as primary beneficiaries along with your STBX. *Note: Some states only allow for your spouse to be listed as the primary beneficiary, not the children.*

It's very common to bundle auto and homeowners insurance together. If you were not involved when setting up those policies, locate your most current policy information which should have been mailed to you. Verify the current deductible, coverage levels, and any specific exclusions to the policy. If you have any trouble finding the policy or have questions on the current coverage, simply call your agent. They can explain everything to you and even mail out a new policy packet. Speaking directly with your agent or customer service allows you to inquire about what your vehicle insurance premiums might be without being bundled, as well as what rental insurance might cost. If the person you're speaking to is not local and does not know you or your STBX, then you can ask as many questions as necessary.

Health and dental insurance is typically offered through either your or your STBX's employer. In that event, you will want to familiarize yourself with each of the policies, including deductibles, copays, coinsurance, in-network and out-of-network providers, coverage limits, and excluded services. You can call insurance companies directly to request additional insurance cards and to inquire when coverage ends, using the example of asking what if the employee leaves their job and/or there's a divorce, and if coverage is related to the date of the occurrence or the end of the month.

If your STBX carries the insurance, check with the human resource department of *your* employer to inquire about the health and dental coverage offered. A divorce is considered a qualifying event and most insurance companies allow you to start coverage right away (in accordance with the employer's criteria). If, for any reason, you cannot obtain coverage through your employer's group plan, then you will need to start researching individual policies for the future.

Personal Property Assets

Many people think of their personal property assets as only the large-ticket things, like a house, land, or a vehicle. This is actually a pretty extensive category, but we'll start out with the big stuff first and then drill down into the less obvious items.

Your home, land, vacation property, rental property, time shares—If you own your home or any additional properties, you should have documents showing the assessed value and what you pay for property taxes. These should be with your income tax documents. It's important to know the most current appraised value of your home and any other marital property as well. Locate the documents from the bank or title company that disclose how much your property was last valued for, and the most current tax bill. Your home and any marital property will need to be divided as part of the divorce settlement. We'll talk more about this later on.

Vehicles, motorcycles, campers, recreational vehicles (boats, ATVs, snowmobiles, jet skis, and trailers), farm equipment, lawn tractors, etc.—Locate any titles, VIN numbers, license information, and/or sales receipts. Find the model (name or number), the year it was manufactured, etc. Make note of the current mileage (or hours used), as well. You can also look for the insurance documents for these details and/or call your insurance agent.

Go online and research the current value of these items. You can look at Kelly Blue Book values for many of the items, or call dealerships who sell them to inquire about the potential value should you wish to sell outright or trade it in. Knowing the current value of this personal property will be necessary when negotiating the division of items and for the divorce settlement.

Gifts and inheritances—These items typically stay with the person who was gifted them and are not considered marital property. However, an exception may be considered regarding inheritance in the event you commingle money (e.g., you use the $10,000 inheritance to build a fancy workshop on your marital property or use it as a down payment to purchase your marital residence). Please consult your divorce attorney, as laws may differ by state.

It's important to know the current and potential value of both your appreciating and depreciating assets. What's key is to be completely transparent with your attorney about them, as you want an even and fair playing field when it comes to sorting out all the details in the divorce.

At the end of this chapter, I will share an important "to-do" as it pertains to identifying the rest of your personal property assets. But first we'll discuss debts and loans.

Debts and Loans

To have a crystal-clear picture of your marital financial situation, it's critical to know all of your debts, total amounts outstanding, repayment terms, and monthly payments. This includes mortgage, second mortgage, home equity loans, vehicle and recreational vehicle loans, credit cards and store cards (their current balances, interest rates, and monthly payment amounts), liens on your property (from the bank or a title loan), money due back to a cash advance/ money store, student loans, and any loans you and/or your STBX have cosigned on. These debts will need to be included when completing the financial disclosure form for your divorce.

Ideally, during this time, before you leave, consider paying down as much debt as possible, starting with high-interest credit cards and loans. Be careful, though, as your STBX may take the extra space on credit cards as his invitation to charge more or to take out a loan for a new toy. You don't want to get stuck potentially having to pay half of his new boat payment during your divorce process, for example. Typically, courts will split credit card debt equally between the divorcing parties, but tend to assign the debts for vehicles and recreational vehicles to the person who uses it most. Laws may differ by state, so be sure to consult your divorce attorney on the division of marital debts.

Do a Home Inventory

Early in my career working in health insurance, I was required to get my Health & Life Insurance License. To maintain my state license I had to take continuing education class's bi-annually. One class I signed up for was called "Risk Management," which was a nice overview of things you can do to reduce your risk of accidents and injuries at home that could result in a small insurance claim for damage or a large claim for, say, a house fire.

One thing that really stuck with me was the idea of doing a home inventory. The instructor talked about how that was crucial if you ever had a fire, because you would need to give a list of all the contents of the house that were lost in the fire in order to claim them. His suggestion was to use a video recorder and go through your entire house. Look in every room, even inside closets, cabinets, dressers, drawers, storage areas, boxes, etc. This included the basement, attic, the garage, and outside the house. I recommend that you do this, too.

When you have finished video recording everything, then sit down and create a spreadsheet that lists all of the items in each room. Yes, every item! Also include, to the best of your ability, what everything cost—what you paid for it, where you bought it, and the approximate year you purchased the item. If you aren't sure of the value of something on your list, search online and put down the current price. As you can imagine, once you're in the midst of this project, you'll quickly realize just how much stuff you own. It's staggering!

The point of doing a home inventory is to have on record all of the marital property. What tends to happen when couples split and get divorced is that some men will remove from the premises expensive items like tools, power tools and equipment, and collectibles. In addition, they may also have a family member or friend hold onto their golf clubs, ski/snowboarding equipment, and hunting and fishing items and gear—guns, expensive rods/reels, binoculars, gun scopes, archery equipment, taxidermy mounts, etc. Why? First, because they know how expensive those items are, and second because in their mind it's all "their" stuff, not yours. They know what it's actually worth, just like women know what certain brand-name purses and shoes are worth. In the grand scheme of things, it's not that you want to take their stuff, but rather you want everything to be looked at fairly when the divorce process starts.

The same holds true with any collectibles (yours or his), such as coins, jewelry, antiques, dishes, stamps, high-end purses or shoes, etc.

Having a video also helps refresh your memory later on, especially after you leave and the situation becomes potentially more risky and emotions and stress are running high. With the video, be sure that the date stamp is turned on, and don't be afraid to have several videos for each room, floor, or areas of your home. And don't forget to video whatever is outside.

If you're able, ask a trusted friend or family member to help you understand the brands or models of the things your STBX has, so you can do the proper research and document their estimated value.

The home inventory also enables you to identify what personal property you might want to take with you when you leave.

You can download a handy checklist to help you through the action steps in this chapter by going to www.ijustwantoutbook.com.

Chapter 6

Step 3: Evaluate Your Current Situation

Where You Are Now

Now that you've read the previous chapter, and hopefully completed as many of the steps that pertain, I have a hunch you might be feeling confident and eager, or nervous and exhausted by all the work you've done so far. Or you might be shifting between the two ends of the spectrum. I assure you that you are exactly where you need to be at this point.

There is no *right* speed in completing the FREEDOM Framework™ process. It's very individual. Completing the entire process may take a couple of years. It may take you one year. Or it could take six months or three months. There are so many variables that can have an effect, but it's not the amount of time that matters. What matters is that you are following the process to figure things out and carefully getting your ducks in a row so that you can get out safely. It personally took me 18 months, but I've had clients who have worked through the process in as little as three months.

Build Your Support Network

In an earlier chapter I advised you not to tell anyone yet about your plans to leave your marriage. By keeping this close to your chest, per se, it has allowed you to get clearer in your mind about your decision, free of being swayed by any outsider opinions or influence. I have a hunch you've already been assessing individuals and have a good idea who you can trust and who will stand by you through this process, all while keeping it secret. The time has come to build your support network.

Confiding in trusted friends and family members is an important step in the process. You will benefit from having support along the way, and even nudging or reassurance if you find yourself stuck. Your confidants can assist by doing fieldwork and additional research, and they can also help maintain the "status quo" during get-togethers to keep your STBX from catching on to anything.

I began building my support network slowly. It started with a few close friends, followed by my family. I invited two of my closest girlfriends to lunch one day, telling them there was something I wanted to get their opinion about. Those ladies had each met my STBX and were already aware things hadn't been perfect in my marriage, and they loved and supported me. I shared details about my STBX's behavior and many of the experiences I had had. Their response was a resounding, "Girl, you need to get the hell out of that craziness!" When I told them

I was getting things in order to leave him but it was going slower than I had anticipated, they eagerly asked how they could help. That felt good!

Next up was talking to my family, initially my parents and then my siblings, to make them aware of what had been going on and of my decision. Thanks to time and many learning experiences, my parents cared far less about what others thought any longer. I felt fortunate my entire family was on board with my decision and said they'd gladly help me with any of my planning.

What seemed to make the greatest difference was how I spoke to my friends and family. I was calm and confident in my decision to leave my marriage and I wasn't reeling in the drama or acting like a martyr. I had things thought through, shared what I had figured out so far, and simply asked for their moral support. What I got in turn was so much more.

My support network helped scout potential areas to move to, rental prices, new school options, getting estimates on personal property values, as well as helping me on moving day—which we will discuss in more detail in this and the upcoming chapters.

Leaving Versus Keeping Your House

A big decision to make is whether to leave your marital home or stay and have your STBX leave. Everyone's circumstances are different, and—much like you did with envisioning staying in or leaving the marriage—I invite you to do the same with your home. (This book details the steps for leaving your home, but if you feel strongly about staying then I recommend you discuss that option with your divorce attorney.)

The idea of leaving your home can seem scary, even at this point. You've invested time, sweat equity, and money into this house. It's where you've created many memories, and may be the only home your kids have known. I totally get it! All that you've done to create a *home* for your family wasn't a waste. What makes a home is the love that comes from within you. It's that state of comfort and connection people feel when they're around you and the safety your kids know and rely on. *That* feeling can be created wherever you live and isn't representative of a specific dwelling or mailing address.

Moving from your marital home provides you a fresh start and the opportunity to move on with your life. You get to decide where you want to live that best fits with your dreams and those you have for your children. You can select to live closer to your job and in a better school district with more opportunities for your children.

Staying in your marital home may make it more difficult to cut the cord with your STBX. The biggest issue will be trying to get him to leave, which will create even more drama because if he didn't physically harm you there are no grounds for him to have to leave. Plus he'll feel he can come and go from the house whenever he wants, stating that he has the right because he still owns it, or he may even be inclined to stalk you when you have the kids. Also, depending on the age of the house, you may get saddled with a money pit or a mortgage payment you cannot afford alone. In many cases, cutting your losses is the smart way to go.

When to Leave

Deciding the best time to leave will depend on a variety of factors. This can include the ages of your children, their school schedules, and their extra-curricular activities. It may also be impacted by your schedule, which will be discussed more in this chapter, as well as your STBX's schedule, which we'll cover in Chapter 8.

I personally chose to move mid-summer because it created the least amount of conflict with my young kids' schedules. It was summer break from school and my boys were not involved in any sports or activities. It was also when I knew my STBX would be gone more working his second job.

As stated earlier, you do not need to rush the planning process. What's more important is to be fully prepared in advance of leaving.

Job Status and Income

It's very important to have a reliable job, something that will enable you to support yourself and your kids once you leave. Ideally it would be a full-time position with daytime hours that work well with your kids' school-year schedules.

Assess your current job to determine if it provides a suitable income level and consider whether you are happy in your position. Know that your divorce process could take six months to a year, and you will want a job you can rely on and that allows flexibility and adequate vacation or personal days for appointments with an attorney and for court dates. If you've worked in your position for some time and you feel you can sit tight, then do that. Trying to juggle a job change in the midst of leaving your marriage and getting divorced may be too stressful, and could potentially impact the on boarding process and learning of your new responsibilities.

However, if you find yourself in a situation where you need a better job or different position, make that transition first. This could be an internal job change with the same company or securing a new position that offers flexibility for any appointments with your attorney or court hearings. Ideally, you will want to consider a new position in the community you're considering moving to. This new position doesn't necessarily have to be a "forever" type of job, just something that supports your decision to move closer to work when you leave.

If need be, you can look for a temporary job, but be sure to tell them that you do not wish to be considered for hire by the new employer and that you want to keep your options open. A temp job will give you the flexibility in the event you cannot report to work due to court issues, etc., without harming your reputation with a full-time permanent employer. If questioned by a future employer about why you worked for a temp agency, you can simply tell them then that you were going through a divorce and needed a job that was more flexible during that time.

If you already have a full- or part-time job, inform your boss and possibly human resources of your personal situation and your plans to leave. Being up-front and honest will allow for understanding if you need additional time off of work and hopefully more flexibility with your schedule. If you are slated for an annual raise, depending on how much it is, you may want to ask your employer to delay it until your divorce is final. Ideally, you want your income to be less than or equal to your STBX's, if possible. You don't want to find yourself having to pay him child support or maintenance/alimony.

Continuing Education

If you are currently enrolled in a college degree program, it may be in your best interest to delay completing your degree until after your divorce is final. If at all possible, take a sabbatical, or reduce your classes to part-time. If you do end up completing all of your required classes, you can simply speak to your advisor to request to hold off on graduating until after your divorce is final. The college may be able to accommodate your request or offer another option, such as pursuing a second major, which can delay your graduation and offer you more career opportunities in the future. Being enrolled in college may positively influence the judge's perception of you, and he/she may opt to award extra financial support to offset your current income if it's significantly lower than your STBX's.

If you've dreamed of returning or going to college, you may wish to wait until after your divorce is finalized. First, you will have your hands full with leaving, the divorce process, and starting your new life. Check to see if your employer offers education assistance or tuition reimbursement, and, if so, what the terms are of that benefit. In addition, once you are divorced you are considered a single parent and the chances of qualifying for scholarships, grants, and higher amounts of financial aid improves because only your income is considered, versus a household income if you're married.

Many women choose to go back to school after they're divorced. It's a great opportunity and can help in creating your new life. It also fills time and offers other things to focus on, especially when the kids are away with the other parent. I suggest waiting until you feel the dust has settled from your divorce so you can better focus on selecting the degree program that best fits with your dreams, so you're better able to focus on your studies.

At the time of my divorce, I had a Bachelor's degree, but my STBX only had a college certificate. The court ruled that I had a higher earning potential because of my higher degree. And because I was in my early 30s and four years younger than my STBX, I had more earning years ahead of me than he did. All of which reduced the amount of the monthly child support award granted to me. Five years after divorcing, I was ready to advance my education to pursue my Master's degree. I was fortunate to qualify for student loans because I was a single parent with a lower household income.

Medical and Dental Procedures

In a previous chapter you researched the health and dental insurance coverage you or your STBX carries. Knowing your insurance and coverage can help you plan for any necessary medical or dental procedures for yourself or your kids before you leave. This would include routine medical, dental, and vision exams, follow-up visits with a specialist, surgery (medically necessary and elective), dental procedures, purchasing new glasses or contacts, and even orthodontia treatment for the kids. Starting (or completing) these services before leaving your marriage can help ensure there will be adequate coverage for that, as well as any necessary recovery or healing time. Purchasing vision hardware, medical supplies, or prescriptions in larger quantities may also allow for insurance coverage as well as provide additional time before you have to purchase them on your own or deal with splitting kid expenses with your STBX.

If your kids are in need of it and at the appropriate age for it, consider starting their orthodontia treatments before you leave. With this treatment underway, your STBX will not be able to get out of helping pay his half of the expenses for it during and after the divorce process. That monthly expense (if there's a payment plan) will be part of what the court orders be split by the parents. Again, be sure to know what your dental insurance covers and discuss payment options with the orthodontia provider before those services begin. Depending on the state you reside in and the insurance policy, your STBX may not be able to terminate you or the kids from his policy until the divorce is final. The same holds true if you carry the insurance.

As a reminder, when you leave be sure to have the most current insurance cards. If you don't have access to the policy information, you can request that a packet be sent to you at home from the insurance company, or get access to view it online. You should also be able to ask questions of the benefits staff at your STBX's employer if the insurance company cannot answer them.

Find out when your coverage will terminate—will it be terminated on the date of your divorce or at the end of the month? In the event your STBX carries the insurance through his work, he'll most likely be ordered to continue insuring the kids after your divorce. You will need to obtain insurance through your employer, but if that's not an option you *may* qualify for state health insurance as a single parent depending on your current income.

Following my divorce, I had access to my employer's health and dental insurance, but was court-ordered to carry the dental for my kids. My ex was court-ordered to carry the medical for the kids, but chose to also carry dental. At the time of our divorce, our kids were not old enough for orthodontia, but a few years later we were able to utilize the insurance coverage from each of our dental plans to offset the out-of-pocket expenses for phase one of their braces.

Personal Property

As you evaluate your current situation, I invite you to begin looking over your personal property to decide what you might want and need to take with you when you leave. Is there enough furniture that you could split it and take the basics while still leaving items for your STBX? The same would hold true with TVs, kitchen items, home décor, and basic cleaning and yard tools. In the event you don't have enough to split up evenly or you don't care for those items, then you can purchase them elsewhere, either new or secondhand.

I enjoyed planning the move and envisioning what our future would look like without all of the stress, and how it would feel to finally be free. I was able to split most of the household items easily, except the kids' things. I chose to take all of their furniture, clothes, and toys along when I left, as I knew I wouldn't be able to get anything left behind once we moved out. I sorted through their toys afterward and sent back things they wanted to play with at their dad's house. My family loaned me a bed and a kitchen table, and bought me new cookware and curtains, which helped a lot. I found that having familiar furniture, décor, and house wares helped my boys feel more comfortable in our new home.

Vehicle

Having a reliable vehicle is probably essential. Consider the vehicle you have, the age and its current condition. Are you making monthly loan or lease payments? Regardless, be sure the payments are something you can afford on your own later. You may wish to trade your vehicle for a newer one that has a good reputation for reliability and lower maintenance and insurance costs. New and certified newer vehicles tend to offer lower interest rates that you can pay directly to the auto manufacturer, such as Toyota. Depending on the time of year, you may also benefit from a low payment lease option.

A loan payment isn't bad and can actually assist you when the court considers each party's current debts. If you have a higher interest rate, you may wish to refinance with a different lender, or inquire about the possibility of changing your payment terms. In the event you can pay off your auto loan balance now, do that, as it can reduce your monthly bills later. If you receive a financial settlement out of your divorce, you can always pay it off then.

If your vehicle is in need of any repairs or general maintenance, insist that be taken care of, even if it means you have to take it into the shop alone. Things to consider include new tires, filters, and belts, as vehicle warranties don't typically cover these items. Watch for coupons or discount promotions, call to compare prices, or ask a car-savvy family member or friend for advice. If need be, you can tell your STBX your vehicle was making a very weird sound and you were worried it was something serious so you took it in right away. This is one of those "ask for forgiveness after the work is completed" versus "asking for permission first" situations.

Another thing to look into is your vehicle's title. If it says "or" (e.g., your name *or* STBX's name), you can easily trade or sell the vehicle. Titles that list "and" (e.g., your name *and* STBX's name) will require your STBX's signature before you will be allowed to trade or sell the vehicle. If you decide to upgrade your vehicle before leaving, that would be the perfect time to change the "and" to "or."

Managing the Managing

Whew. Those are a lot of details to explore and to manage. The good news is that you don't need to do it all in the same week—or even the same year. What's important when dealing with the issues in this chapter is to take your time and really think about each item discussed before you take action.

You can download a handy checklist to help you through the action steps in this chapter by going to www.ijustwanoutbook.com.

Evaluating your current situation in this way will continue to lay the necessary foundation for being better prepared to stand on your own. The next chapter will help you move forward even further in protecting yourself financially and legally.

Chapter 7

Step 4: Exercise Your Rights

Years of dealing with an abusive and controlling spouse can leave you feeling as though you have no rights. The great news is every step in the FREEDOM Framework™ process is an investment in your and your kids' future. You have every legal right to protect yourself and to ensure you can get out safely and are made financially whole in accordance with state laws. In this chapter we'll look at additional ways for you to do that.

Bank Account and Major Credit Card

Opening up your own bank accounts (checking and savings) and taking out a major credit card (Visa, MasterCard, Discover, etc.) are crucial steps before you leave. The bank accounts and credit card should only be in your name. With the convenience of mobile and online banking, you don't have to worry about having monthly statements or bills mailed home. Simply have them emailed to your new secret email account. You can open this new account at the same bank, *but do not link it to your other accounts*. Keep it separate so you don't tip off your STBX!

In the event you have a side business, it's necessary to keep your business money separate versus commingling it with your personal accounts. It's also easier to manage money from a business account when you're purchasing inventory and supplies. Plus, your tax accountant will advise you to have a separate account for income tax purposes.

A few years before I left, I became an independent sales consultant for a national direct-sales company doing in-home parties. I really enjoyed getting out of the house and meeting new people, plus I did quite well financially.

I was able to use my side business as my excuse to open up separate checking and savings accounts and to get a credit card. My STBX did not like it at first, but as my inventory orders and sales ramped up he saw the value in my not using household money to cover expenses. Unbeknownst to him, any profits I made from my business were quickly tucked away in my business savings account to put towards the security deposit on my rental home, and for purchasing household items after we moved out. All my STBX knew was that I was staying under the income threshold our tax accountant advised so we wouldn't have to pay additional income tax. (Note that you will need to disclose any business profits earned on the financial disclosure form you'll file during the divorce.)

You may want to consider cancelling any store credit card accounts you no longer use. In doing so, you limit the risk of your STBX charging items to create debt that's tied to your name, and you'll reduce the chances of identity theft.

Payroll Direct Deposit

On work paydays you probably receive a check stub or email showing your most recent payroll deposit into your personal bank account. Now that you have a new checking account, contact the payroll department to find out how to change your direct-deposit account and how long it takes to switch from one bank account to another. Use that information to plan when to shift your paycheck deposit from the household account to your new bank account.

Many larger employers allow you to make the change online and it can be done between pay periods. Others may require you to first submit a form, but there may be a waiting period before the change can go through. Be sure to have your bank's routing number and your new account number handy when you set up the change. Coordinate when to switch your payroll deposits to your new account so it happens just before or immediately after you leave.

Safety Deposit Box

Safety deposit boxes may seem old-fashioned, but they are quite useful and definitely secure. You can rent one at your bank and use it to store any of the original (or copies of) paperwork for the divorce or paperwork for your future residence, such as the rental agreement. In addition, if you have any stashed cash, that can be kept in there, too.

Assign a trusted family member or friend to share access to your safety deposit box. Should something happen to you, your assigned person can go to the bank, retrieve all the documentation from the box, and get it to your attorney for proper handling. That trusted person will need to go with you to your bank to be added. They'll need to present their driver's license or state-issued ID and sign some paperwork—the process takes about 15 minutes to complete. Remember to keep the safety deposit box key hidden from your STBX.

If you're unable to get a safety deposit box, then simply ask a trusted family member or friend to store your items in a fireproof safe (which you can get at an office supply store) at their home. Know that the person you select to hold your items must remain discreet.

Cell Phone

Having a reliable cell phone—ideally a smartphone—is important so you have access to the Internet wherever you go. This may require you to upgrade your phone with your current provider or change cell carriers to benefit from their new customer discounts and offerings. Having a sizable data plan can help offset the need for Internet at your future residence, at least initially.

Your planned departure date may not line up with your current cell plan contract, but don't let that affect when you plan to leave. If your STBX is the account holder and you don't have the ability to make changes, or you'd rather just be off on your own, then research a new cell plan, even with a different carrier, and inquire about getting a new number. This will enable you to get a brand-new phone number. Most carriers have very attractive plans when you're a brand-new customer. If your STBX is the primary on your cell plan and you're not under a contract, he may try to have your line disconnected as soon as you leave and you'll be without a phone.

If the account is in your name primarily, you can have future bills emailed to your new secret email address. Wait to update your new mailing address until the divorce process is in full swing, and remember to change your sign-on and password so your STBX can't hack into the account. Before leaving, recycle any old paper copies of cell phone bills as he may look at the numbers dialed to investigate who you've been calling. And if it's possible, remove your STBX from having the ability to make any changes on the account, including getting a new phone or having that new phone billed to the account. If that happens you'll end up paying for his new phone on the next bill.

After you're safely out, you can go into the cell store and fill out paperwork allowing your STBX's phone line to be separated from the account so he can be on his own. Know that he may not wish to comply until after the divorce is final, sticking you with the monthly payment for his usage. You can request that your STBX reimburse you for his portion each month. Refusals to reimburse or any intentional overuse by your STBX may be included in the divorce settlement so you can be made whole.

If you cannot afford a new smartphone, then purchase a burner phone, such as a TracFone or a similar brand. This can be easily purchased from Wal-Mart or other big box retailers. It's about getting a new phone number so you can safely communicate about your upcoming departure.

Obviously, you would want to hide your phone and only use it when your STBX (and the kids) are not around. When it's stored, keep the ringer turned off. To help keep suspicion lower, pay cash for the burner phone and consider getting the same type of phone you already have with the same cover in the event you accidentally leave it around or he digs through your purse. Start using the burner phone for outgoing and incoming calls about your moving-out plans—the new rental place, the movers, daycare, school, etc.

Or, depending on the type of job you have and your responsibilities, you can say it's your new work phone.

In addition, be mindful of when you have your GPS tracking enabled or when your sim card is inserted in your phone, as that can be an opportunity for a suspicious STBX to monitor your whereabouts without your knowledge. You will also benefit from doing additional research on cell phone spy apps and software so your activities cannot be tracked by your STBX.

Retirement Plans and Payroll Contributions

During the research and documentation step you had the pleasure of getting reacquainted with your retirement accounts. Based on your research you should have an idea of how much you and your STBX each have in your retirement funds. What are the amounts? Do you have more or does your STBX? Answers to those questions can affect what's next.

At any time, you have the ability to turn off retirement contributions, either through a current work-sponsored 401k or 403b or a separate IRA. This can be temporary until your divorce is finalized. Know that whatever amount you have in your retirement accounts may be up for grabs in the divorce settlement—meaning that if you have more in retirement than your STBX, he may have the right to half of your retirement savings added during the time you were legally married. By ceasing contributions, you are lowering the amount of money he may be entitled to. The same is true if your STBX has more money in his retirement than you.

Another option is to cash in any IRAs. This can be done to equalize with the amount your STBX has, if his are lower. You can also use the money to pay down any debts you don't want to get stuck with in the divorce or to fund your departure—to pay for deposits on your future home or apartment, for your attorney retainer fee and any additional divorce fees, or to hire outside support, such as a life coach.

Know that cashing in retirement funds while you are still legally married will increase the total household income, and at tax time you may have to pay more or not get as much back from a tax return. Also, there will be fees and penalties deducted from the total amount in your account.

To reduce issues with your income taxes, simply have any federal and state taxes taken out up-front. Your check will be for the remaining balance after taxes, penalties, and fees are deducted. Please consult with your investment representative for further details.

Be advised that your STBX has the legal right to cash in his IRAs, as well, so be prepared for the unexpected. During my divorce process, my STBX cashed in his IRA because he didn't want me to get his money. The downside was he never had taxes deducted at the time of the withdrawal so we took a huge hit on our tax return and I was legally responsible for half of the un-taxed income (our attorneys instructed we file jointly during our divorce process). In the end, I decided not to go after half of his 401k account because that balance was equal to what I had in my retirement accounts.

Research and Interview Divorce Attorneys

The time has come to exercise your right to legal representation. Provide yourself ample time to research divorce attorneys. Ask your support network to help come up with a list of potential lawyers to contact. They can ask around anonymously on your behalf, and maybe even search online for bios and share that information with you.

There are a variety of things to consider. Most of all, you'll want an attorney who is experienced with handling divorces, who you feel you can trust, and who is willing to work for your case and for you. Here's a list of criteria to look for and potential questions to ask:

- How long has the attorney been practicing?
- What is their experience level with divorce cases?
- What's their experience and interest in representing a client who has been emotionally abused?
- What is their current retainer fee and hourly rate thereafter?
- What is their current caseload? Do they have space and time in their caseload to take you on?

- Will they have another attorney or paralegal assisting them? If so, is that person exclusive or do they support other attorneys too?
- How well does the attorney know other attorneys, the judges in your county, and guardian ad litem (if one is assigned)?

Ideally, meet with each attorney face-to-face for a free consultation. But if that's not an option, set up a phone interview. You do not need to disclose during the conversation that you're planning to leave. If possible, during an in-person consultation, request a copy of the divorce process financial disclosure form and ask if they could explain what is typically needed for each category, and how in-depth you need to get.

Base your decision on the interview and how you feel when speaking with each attorney. If something feels off, exclude that person as an option or put them at the bottom of your list and move on to the next one. It's best not to hire an attorney on impulse or only on other's recommendations. Meet them and then decide who you feel best fits your needs.

Stay away from the barracuda types or those who brag about what they can get you in the end, as they tend to overpromise and under-deliver, leaving you with a hefty bill in the end far exceeding what you anticipated. Initially, they may seem like the ideal attorney, but what you could wind up with is someone who is all about threats and intimidation games trying to incite dramatic reactions out of your STBX. I understand after all the years of turmoil with your abusive spouse that you may see this as the way to get back at and punish him, but I assure you all the antics will only piss off the court and result in additional expenses. The unnecessary drama will also trickle down and negatively affect your kids from the added stress they're exposed to from you and your STBX throughout the divorce process.

You don't necessarily need to hire an attorney in advance of leaving, *but I highly recommend it.* You do not need to ask the attorney's permission to leave your marriage abruptly, but you can share your game plan and ask him/her to advise you of your rights and if there are any potential legal ramifications. Simply presenting yourself in a transparent way and honestly telling him/her the truth—that you've suffered emotional abuse, you want what's best for your kids, and you want to be fair and reasonable—will show you are compassionate, despite all of what's happened. The attorneys worth considering are those who appreciate the fact that you have a plan, that you have many things taken care of already, and that you're willing to work as a team with them through the divorce, which will help make their job easier.

Lining Up Your Options

You can download a handy checklist to help you through the action steps in this chapter by going to www.ijustwantoutbook.com.

Rather than view the to-do items in this chapter with fear, see if you can keep your perspective on how *doing these things is a way of taking care of yourself.* Setting up a new bank account, knowing when to switch your direct deposit, having an additional safe place to store any paperwork, addressing your retirement plan options, and selecting an attorney are all major accomplishments in your journey to freedom.

It's the traveling that gets you to the new and better place, and every step counts.

In the next chapter we'll address exit strategy.

Chapter 8

Step 5: Design Your Exit

Congratulations! You are over halfway through the FREEDOM Framework™ process. Now that you have more things set up and you've spoken to attorneys, you may be feeling overwhelmed by the magnitude of your decision to leave. It is huge! Escaping your abuser is *the* bravest thing you may ever experience.

Imagine for a moment that everything you've read so far in this book has been completed and checked off the list. Look at everything you've accomplished so far. How might you be feeling? I have a hunch you'll be filled with confidence and feeling optimistic about what's to come.

The primary objective is to get out of your abusive marriage and this chapter will walk you through designing your safe exit.

Staying on Course

As you push forward and your support network is more exposed to the details of your plan, some may have their own level of "OMG, this is really happening!" reactions. The reality of the potential danger to you or others if you are found out may cause members of your support network to begin to have doubts, and you may find yourself in the position of being their emotional support. The closer your support network is to the gory details at the center of the fire, the easier it is for them to worry and express their fears, especially if you've been hyper-focused on executing this plan.

I totally get it. I remember using my fear to fuel me to keep everything moving forward. I had to remind my support network that the risk was well worth the reward of getting out safely and swiftly, and how much I appreciated their help and that I needed them to stay on course.

Scout Out Rental Options

The first thing to consider is deciding where you want to move to. Would you like to live in a new city or a different area of your current city? Do you want to be closer to work so your commute is less? Select somewhere that feels really good to you. If at all possible move to a new city (or area) that's at least a 30 to 60 minute drive away from your STBX.

A secret I learned was to look for a rental that offers similar or better amenities as the marital home so it's a new home your kids would like coming to, and for which the monthly rent (or lease payment) is the same or more than your current monthly mortgage payment. In doing so, you may eliminate any responsibility to have to pay your STBX for even a portion of the marital house payment and household bills.

Look around the neighborhoods for places where there are other kids of similar ages so yours can make new friends and have others to play with. Ideally, move to a nicer and safer residential area. You can certainly contact a rental finder company, talk with a realtor, or get help from your support network to do research. Talk to people who live in those potential areas and nonchalantly ask them what they like/dislike, and if they know of any available rentals.

Don't be afraid to be picky and do not hesitate to avoid areas that look sketchy, because that may not be very safe for you or your kids. Plus, your STBX could use that against you during the divorce in attempts to reduce the amount of placement time you have with the kids. Where you live may also persuade the court to not allow you primary placement of the kids.

In my situation, I moved to the city within five miles of my job. I was fortunate to find a brand new duplex in a subdivision with families with kids who were about the same age as my kids. We had a nice yard for my boys to play in, a garage to safely park my vehicle in and for storing things, and the convenience of a nearby school bus pick-up zone.

Daycare Changes

At the same time you're scouting potential new rentals, consider daycare and school-changes. For children in daycare (infants, toddlers, and preschool), consider switching them to one that's closer to your work. This is something you can consider months before you leave so that your child can get acclimated before your move. You can justify the reason for the switch to your STBX by saying the kids will be closer to you should they get sick and have to be picked up, plus it's cheaper as they can be at the daycare for less time each day. You can also say that you'll do all the running back and forth so your STBX isn't inconvenienced by the change, which can also help reduce any suspicion he might have.

If you're unable to switch your kids to a new daycare before you move, then speak confidentially to the daycare manager and explain your situation and your potential plans to switch to a new daycare. The manager might be able to offer a referral to another center in your new community. Plus, if they know in advance that your kids will be leaving, they can better prepare for any potential fallout. Their staff can also be forewarned in case they're questioned by your STBX. Only share that information, though, if you feel confident that they won't share more information with your STBX than you've authorized.

In my situation, I switched my younger son from an in-home babysitter to the daycare at my work about four months before we moved out. This daycare was huge and functioned like a preschool based on the ages of the kids. They had rooms specifically for infants, one-year-olds, two-year-olds, etc. At the start of each new school year (or on their birthday), the kids shifted up to the next room. The daycare also offered a school-age program in the summer months that included learning activities, arts and crafts, reading, exercise activities, and fun field trips.

School Changes

If changing schools fits with your needs, research ones in the areas you're interested in moving to, to help you determine if they are a good fit for your kids. Look for schools that offer more opportunities than your kids' current school—ideally with a higher ranking, a reputation for teaching excellence where your kids can flourish and grow, and one that offers any specific services your child might need. You should be able to search online, ask a realtor, or contact the schools individually to request information. You can call the school to schedule a meeting with the principal or assistant principal and get a tour of the facility. Know that the rankings could differ between elementary, junior high, and high school.

Additional things to consider include whether the school offers a bus service for before and after-school programs. Have your support network help in asking people what they like and dislike about the schools, sports programs, and activities. If public transportation is the only option for your kids, be sure to know the city bus schedules and routes, and have a plan (and a back-up plan) in place for getting your kids to and from school each day.

For junior high or high schools, ask if the schools are more of a college-prep level, or what courses they offer to help prepare kids for college. Also look into their sports programs and extracurricular activities. If the school is an academic step up, that is another legitimate reason to support your wanting the kids to change schools.

Ideally, you'll want your kids to change schools at the start of a new school year. Elementary-age kids are much more resilient to the change and making new friends. Junior high- and high schoolers tend to adjust better when other students are also dealing with the changes of starting at a new school.

When I left my husband, my oldest son had just finished first grade. The primary reason I moved to the community I selected was because of the school district and its great reputation, high state rankings, and excellence in teaching. It was a big step up academically from the former school, and one the court could not dispute the benefits of.

Select Items to Take With You

In Chapter 6 you began assessing your personal property and what items you may want to take when you move. I suspect you have a good idea already of what you intend to move versus what you'll purchase. Once you leave, your STBX will likely not let you back into the house to get anything you forgot or couldn't haul during the move. Plus it might be more dangerous to come back later and try to get stuff.

In January of 2002, six months before I moved out, I went through all of our household things that were in storage under the guise that I wanted to purge stuff we no longer needed and finally organize everything else that we wanted to keep. I sorted everything into piles for garage sale, donation items, trash, and things to keep.

I bought new storage bins and labeled them with detailed content descriptions for those things I wanted to hold onto and shelved the bins for quick access. I even went so far as to have extra bins and separated out certain home and holiday décor that I knew I didn't want to take along. From there, I worked on prepping all the items for the garage sale.

In May, I had a huge garage sale and sold a ton of stuff, including what was left of my boys' baby clothes and toys they had outgrown. I split the sale earnings between our household account, my secret new bank account, and the kids' savings accounts. What didn't sell was donated.

You can organize boxes in storage that you don't want to take along and separate them out from those you do. Simply put them on different shelves, or leave a space between the areas so you don't have to sort through them on moving day, as that will take time.

Purging and organizing really helped me evaluate what I was going to take and what would be left behind. I even helped my STBX go through the garage and his storage shed in the backyard to find items for the garage sale. It was perfect for getting a look at what we had and I was able to take a mental inventory of what additional items I might need to take along.

If you don't have the opportunity to dig through everything, you can take pictures or use the video from your home inventory to select the items you want to take when you move.

You can also take boxes along when you move and then sort through them after you've moved and return anything that belongs to your STBX or things you don't want or need.

Letting Go Of Attachments

The Internet is filled with articles and websites that talk about the benefits of letting go of attachments—to people, things, and places. It's easier said than done, but it *is* attainable. Here's how. Simply start by making a deliberate withdrawal of emotional investment in what once was, such as personal items, routines, and your home.

Attachments to Personal Items—The sorting, evaluating, purging, and selling phase can really assist in letting go of attachments to tangible things. For me, it felt like a mental cleansing knowing that I wasn't obligated to take any of the awful gifts received from my crazy mother-in-law over the years, nor would I have to look at any of the memorabilia or collections my STBX had that I couldn't stand. There was a great freedom in secretly selecting exactly what I wanted and needed. It honestly felt like the noose was loosening around my neck finally.

Attachments to Your Routines—There's one thing about routines—they can be annoying and frustrating—especially when you feel trapped having to follow a control freak's routine in order to keep peace and risk getting raged at if you or the kids unintentionally interfere with it. Knowing there was an end in sight in having to deal with his routine helped me be more patient. Plus, I found easy workarounds. For example, on Sundays when I did laundry I planned out the boys' outfits for the upcoming week and stacked them on the shelf in their closet for quick retrieval on weekday mornings. The kids helped me set out their breakfast dishes the night before. After they were dressed I allowed them to watch a kids' show while they ate breakfast at the table and I got ready. I also started taking my shower in the evening and setting my clothes out for the next day. Those few simple changes kept the boys from accidentally triggering their dad in the morning, and allowed me and the boys to get out the door in a fraction of the time, even after we moved out.

Attachments to Your Home—As I mentioned in a previous chapter, where you live is only a structure. What makes a *home* is what you create, and that goes with you wherever you move to. In the month prior to leaving, I allowed myself time to slowly say good-bye to the house I had put so much time and sweat equity into. I went through each of the rooms and took time to appreciate the memories, from the transformation during remodeling and decorating, to special occasions spent with my kids, and with friends and family for get-togethers. I physically touched every part of the house. I gave it all the love I could, knowing it was time to move on to a new opportunity.

Pick a Moving Date

This decision may need to be in the works for some time. Select a date that works best with your and your kids' schedules. Most importantly, select a time when you know your spouse will be gone for the entire process, ideally for at least a couple of days or over a weekend. He could be at his primary job working or traveling for work, working at a second job, gone on a hunting or fishing trip, golfing or snowmobile/ATV trip, or enjoying a getaway trip with his buddies. Think about his hobbies, interests, and potential reasons to be gone for a full day, overnight, or an entire weekend. Be supportive if he wants to spend a chunk of money to go do whatever he wants, or buy him a ticket to get out of town. Having this set date is your window of opportunity to organize and plan for it, and then safely get out.

For my STBX's second job as an EMT, he took shifts once a month requiring him to be away overnight for 48 hours in the next town, ten miles away. He selected the weekend shifts he wanted to work for that entire summer ahead of time, so I knew well in advance when he'd be gone.

Select Your New Rental Home

It's time to narrow down your list of potential new rentals and make a final decision. Be sure to ask the landlord for average costs of heating and cooling, sewer, water, and garbage pickup so you can budget those into your monthly expenses. Signing a yearlong lease should give you the best pricing, depending on the landlord or management company. If need be, ask a trusted family member or friend to be your reference on the credit check.

Start your lease a few weeks to a month before you move out. This will enable you to have access to your rental and help you finalize the list of furniture and personal belongings you want to take when you move. It will also allow you to make sure utilities are up and running by the time you move in, to plan the layout of your rooms, and to have a place to start tucking away items you buy on the side or which family and friends loan to you.

As soon as you take on the rental, set up your basic utilities. You can schedule the cable and internet installation a couple of days before you move in, or wait until later and use your cell phone data plan in the interim. If you cannot be present for the installation, recruit someone from your support network to be there. You can request to pay for the installation in advance, or have your friend fill out a pre-signed check.

Updating Your Address

As you are getting your rental set up and turning on utilities you will obviously only give them your new address. Set up your new utilities to email your bills and to do online bill pay. You can easily file an address change—either online, over the phone, or in person—for the bank accounts and credit cards that are only in your name. Updating your address versus officially forwarding your mail will keep your new address secret from your STBX. It will also save you from receiving junk mail at your new home.

Hire a Moving Company

While it might seem more risky having a big truck in your driveway on moving day, a moving company will be the fastest way to get all of the things you want to take out of your house and delivered to your new rental. They can save lots of time and backbreaking work carrying furniture and boxes. Depending on how far away you are moving, the entire moving process can take as little as four hours. It is well worth the investment to get you out fast! You can inquire about what times of day (including evening, middle of the night, midday) they are available, as that might help with your moving needs.

Recruit your support network to save boxes that can be used for packing. Have them show up on moving day to help pack boxes and carry them to the garage (or loading zone) so the movers can quickly load when they arrive.

Think about all the areas of your house you will be removing items from, and the contents in each room, then assign one to two people per area. You can make lists for each of the rooms that you can give your packing crew on moving day. (More on this in Chapter 10.)

At your new rental, take time to label each of the rooms (e.g., master bedroom, bedroom 2, etc.) before moving day. This will help the movers and your moving buddies to know where to take boxes and larger items on move-in day. It speeds up the process and saves you money in the event you want the movers to only bring in the heavy items. Boxes can be unloaded into the garage for the moving buddies to carry into your new rental.

Recruit a Babysitter For Moving Day

Depending on the ages and understanding levels of your children, you may want to designate someone to take the kids for a day of fun—to the movies or a trampoline park or arcade, and out for lunch. This will keep them out from underfoot so you can focus on the move, and it will postpone any emotional struggles the kids might experience if they are involved. You don't want your young kids to know in advance about the move because it may cause too much stress and they should not be expected to keep the secret.

Have the kids picked up before the moving buddies and the moving truck arrive. You also don't want the kids to be brought back to you at your new rental until after you are moved in and have most everything set up. It will be stressful enough when you have to tell your kids later that you've moved. This is a good time for a relative to take the kids for two or three days.

Schedule a Vacation From Work For the Week After Moving

Taking vacation will give you time to help the kids settle in, as well as provide ample free time to meet with your attorney. It will also give you time to get more of your personal belongings unpacked, and for you to have a chance to settle in more at your new home.

During this time off work you can take care of any loose ends you weren't able to finish prior to moving, such as updating your address with your physician and dental offices. You can do that over the phone, in person, or make updates online through the medical facilities patient portal. If possible, also update your HIPAA privacy paperwork so that your STBX cannot call to get updates on your healthcare, dental services, or bills. For the kids, be sure you are listed as the responsible party and give the office your new mailing address. This will allow you to manage any medical expenses more easily, and you will then be in charge of your STBX reimbursing you later. Keep copies of all medical bills so you can share those with your attorney.

Update the daycare that you moved so they can be more attentive to your children and let you know of any issues they might be having. It will also enable daycare staff to be prepared to notify you should your STBX show up to try to take the kids when it's not his court-ordered visitation time.

Notify the Police Department

Before moving out you may find it beneficial to let your local police or sheriff's department know what has been going on in your relationship and that you made plans to move out when your STBX is away. Advise them that you have an attorney and that you've hired movers to help get you out as fast as possible. Tell them the time the movers will be there so they can do a drive-by in the event your STBX shows up unexpectedly. After you have left, you can call to let them know you are safely out. That will also help prepare them for any freak-out phone calls your STBX might have upon returning home.

Should You Get a Restraining Order?

I only advocate this if the abuse has escalated and your spouse has threatened you or gotten physical with you recently and you feel your life is in danger. I filed for one due to my STBX threatening to kill all of us in an auto accident when he was driving, five days before my planned move-out day. The next day I went to the county domestic abuse center and spoke with them about the incident. The representatives urged me to get a restraining order and they accompanied me to the courthouse to file for one. Because I already had my plans in place to move out and shared that with the court, I asked that he be served *after* we were successfully out. The sheriff's department did just that. My STBX was served while working at his second job as an EMT. The restraining order hearing was held the following week.

Design With the End In Mind

This chapter about designing your exit involves getting serious about taking care of yourself. Of course some of these steps are scary. If they weren't, you would likely have designed your exit sooner. Please be kind to yourself as you consider the best ways to handle these issues and as you grow into a greater position of strength and readiness for actually leaving. It may seem difficult to continue to wait for your design to take shape in reality, but part of what's happening as you wait is that you are becoming a person capable of taking care of yourself and putting that as a priority.

All of the steps, including the steps of looking at the details and considering the options, will enable you to safely leave from a foundation of greater security.

You can download a handy checklist to help you through the action steps in this chapter by going to www.ijustwantoutbook.com.

Before you leave, we need to look at potential opposition and how to prepare for it.

Chapter 9

Step 6: Prepare For Opposition

Your continued emotional detachment from your soon to-be *past* life will enable you to see things from a different perspective. You've learned to stop giving your power over to your STBX and I'm going to ask that when you stumble—because you probably will—you get back up, and unapologetically take back your power again and keep moving forward.

Even if you've been dancing with doubt allowing your STBX's put-downs and name calling to get to you, know that you are not crazy. What has happened in your past at the hand of your STBX is real, even if outsiders didn't see it. I invite you to stay grounded in who you are and in all the wonderful things you have to offer the world and your children. You are intelligent, compassionate, and caring and, yes, you really can do this.

Your departure is going to be the start of a massive shit-storm, but I'm guessing you already knew this. It's still important to look at this issue of opposition so you get real about what can potentially happen and so you can be better prepared for reactions from others (outside of your trusted support network), when you tell your children, and what you will be up against with your STBX. Going into your departure blindly could otherwise take a terrible toll on you and your children. Preparing for opposition will be well worth it and help you stay focused on your goal of getting out safely.

Division of Friendships

The reality is that you will lose people in the divorce. That's how it goes. Not everyone is going to want to stand by you, and that's completely normal and okay. This can include coworkers, friends, and even family members who were not part of your trusted support network. You may hear rumors later that you were viewed as crazy for wanting to leave after all the years you've invested in the marriage and the negative impact getting divorced will have on your kids, despite the emotional abuse.

To be honest, some of these losses may be welcome, allowing distance from annoying in-laws or those who are quick to judge. Other losses may be painful, like friends you made through your STBX who feel compelled to stick by his side. Know that it's not your job to try to convince others to take your side, so watch your expectations around that. Participating in that behavior will only waste valuable time and emotional energy, and increase the potential risk of you slipping down a rabbit-hole where you feel ashamed and "less than." The truth is that what others think of you is none of your business. So let them think what they want. Those who know *you* will stick around.

The divide may only be temporary for those who feel it's best to create distance, thinking they are staying out of it and assuming that will make it less awkward (but it really doesn't). Then there may be some people who don't know how to handle what their friends are going through, causing them to be more attentive to their spouse and children and thus not be available to you. Others may feel insecure about their own relationship or may be finally able to see that their marriage sucks and realize they have been ignoring the signs, too. Lastly, there may even be a select few who are jealous because they're secretly miserable and wish they had your courage to leave.

You may get questioned by people who are nosy busybodies who feel the need to inject their opinion. A few months after we had moved out, I got cornered in the bread aisle at the grocery store by an acquaintance who thought she knew my STBX better than I did and tried to shame me for leaving him. You have the choice to ignore the nosy folks or respectfully tell them what's happening in your life is none of their damn business. I did the latter.

We've unfortunately been encouraged to put up with extremely frustrating behavior—hearing previous generations of women "diss" about how dumb men are, that they need to be taught how to be husbands and fathers, how it's our role as wives and mothers to accept his *flaws* and turn the other cheek, and maintain the illusion of a happy marriage and family. Even now it's not necessarily ethical mainstream conversation to talk about how empowering and freeing it is to leave a relationship that's not serving us, that's not fulfilling, or that's emotionally abusive. Unless we're a celebrity or power figure, we're conditioned to pretend everything is great so we don't end up with that shameful status of "divorced."

Starting a Divorce Trend

When someone takes the leap of faith to leave their marriage, it can trigger others in their circle to evaluate their current situation and follow suit. What ensues is what can be viewed as a contagious divorce trend.

Imagine for a moment a group of girlfriends who go on a girls' weekend to Las Vegas. They're having a blast, feeling uninhibited and free to let their hair down. During all this fun they realize there is way more to life and they each long for more happiness. They're exhausted by all the pretending in their blah or unhealthy marriages, and all the frustrating and stressful responsibilities that go along with being a parent. Plus, they're sick of how their husband treats them. They long for a life where they can have a fun and fulfilling relationship as well as a family. Their other friend, the one who couldn't make the trip, just got out of her abusive marriage and seems happier than ever now. They want that, too.

Upon their return, one by one, they file for divorce. Their decisions are independent of one another, but were prompted by the collective freedom they experienced together and the newfound happiness they see in their friend who went first. The moral of the story is that, down the road, your actions may trigger a divorce streak and you could be blamed by upset outsiders for putting the idea into the newly single ladies' heads.

Divorce scares the hell out of a lot of people, for various reasons. But when others point fingers and cast blame, it's typically their own insecurities shining through or their own unwillingness to take responsibility for parts they played contributing to the end of their marriage.

Divorce is one of the most empowering and freeing experiences you will ever have, and there's no doubt it evokes ripples of change. Being the person who indirectly influences others to stop settling, to challenge their fears, and to step into a better life isn't a bad thing.

When to Tell Your Kids

In order to keep your plans secret from your STBX, you won't be able to tell your kids in advance, especially if they're young. Asking them to keep a secret of that magnitude would be too much of an emotional burden on them, and they could accidentally tell their dad if they're feeling overwhelmed with worry, or out of spite if they get angry with him. Waiting to tell your kids about getting divorced until after you are safely moved out and settled in your new rental will help reduce the chances of your STBX finding out.

This news will require a heart-to-heart conversation with your kids that will most likely not go perfectly. I suggest you do it privately. Decide whether to speak to your children separately or together depending on their ages. It's your choice if you want to tell them it wasn't safe to keep living with daddy anymore. But if you do, be respectful, as your children love their dad regardless of his behavior. Some critics might view this as bashing their dad, but I disagree. I feel it's better to be completely transparent and honest with your kids regarding issues of safety, regardless of their ages.

I realize that the idea of keeping this from your children might feel horrible, and you may already anticipate them taking the news hard. They may not understand and they will likely ask lots of questions, or feel scared and have crying spells or even anger outbursts. I get it, really, I do. What got me past the guilt and worry was that I knew, deep in my heart, that *not* telling them up-front would be the best option for ensuring our safe departure.

Knowing all that, I invite you to take ample time to think about how you'll go about it, what you might say, and what your kids' anticipated reactions might be. Keep in mind that moving out means their new normal will entail living between two homes.

Don't hesitate to discuss the timing of the talk and your wording with a few members of your trusted support network who also know your kids well, as they may be able to offer different options or perspectives.

Further Down the Path

Statistically, 80 percent of the time the woman files for divorce. The woman typically is the one who decides the marriage is over, and she's more likely to be the one to take action. In a non-abusive marriage, the husband is at least six months, if not more, behind where the wife is emotionally. Sure, he may have felt frustrated during the marriage, but most times the typical husband has been living in a state of denial. In an abusive relationship, the STBX can be so far behind they're not even remotely thinking about divorce as a possibility.

While your STBX may act like he hates you and doesn't want to be in the marriage, he still relies heavily on you to continue to feed him emotionally. This is commonly referred to as "emotional supply" in Borderline or Narcissistic Personality Disorder descriptions.

Your STBX will most likely not see this coming, because you've been so good at acting and maintaining the illusion that everything has been fine. In no particular order, he'll go through the grief cycle—shock, denial, bargaining, and anger. I intentionally left out the phase of "moving on," as that most likely won't happen for some time (usually when they find a new victim to provide their emotional supply).

Despite your STBX's controlling and abusive behavior toward you in the past, be mindful that he's been clueless this was all in the works. You've just pulled the rug out from beneath him and served up his biggest fear—he's been abandoned. Abusers lead a self-fulfilling prophecy lifestyle and have a distorted view of reality. Rarely do they even realize that their behavior is creating deep wounds in their loved one's spirit, or—if they do know that—they simply don't care. The abuser does everything in his power to control you and the family, and to keep everything and everyone tightly controlled, all so he can feel safe.

Your STBX now feels betrayed, sad, scared, angry, lost, hurt, out of control, and filled with rage. He cannot think rationally. His emotions are cycling and peaking, and all he wants is revenge. Expect that he *will* respond with a tidal wave of negativity, and you may see a level of hatred and revenge you've never imagined before. Your job is to ride the waves and try to stay on your surfboard.

Distortion Campaign

During your divorce process, expect that your STBX will make you out to be the villain, the bad mother, the crazy wife, etc. He will play the martyr and spin the stories. Any of his awful past behaviors will suddenly be things you did to him or the kids. He will start a distortion campaign, first with friends and family members, then with the court, and, worse yet, with your children. Initially, my ex-husband said I stole the kids and all of his personal belongings, then it was that I was crazy and stole his money—it went on and on and on.

All of your STBX's accusations will likely be topics of conversation between your and his attorneys and, depending on the nature of the issue, potentially also with the guardian ad litem (if appointed), and the judge as well. You may find yourself in uncharted territory, feeling harshly judged by strangers and filled with a new level of concern realizing those individuals have the power to decide your and your children's futures.

As the accusations roll in, be prepared to defend yourself and prove that those statements are false. The more allegations you and your attorney can show are untrue, unfair, or unreasonable—with supporting evidence—the more likely the accusations will positively influence the outcome of your divorce.

You will have to do your best to let the garbage your STBX and his attorney throw at you roll off your back. Focus your energy on only responding to matters that are important to the case, maintaining a mature and professional demeanor, and modeling healthy behavior. I turned into an ice queen and did not speak or correspond with my STBX about anything beyond the immediate needs of the kids. Yes, it's going to be challenging not to respond to the other stuff, but that's exactly what he'll try to bait you into doing. By not allowing my STBX to pull me into an argument, I protected myself and my kids from the unnecessary drama.

Be alert. Not rising to the bait may trigger your STBX to move onto bigger threats and intimidation tactics, though it's doubtful any will work to his favor in the end. This is when your trusted support network comes in handy, or when a trained coach who specializes in dealing with divorce can be reassuring. They can walk beside you through this process.

Whatever drama happens during your divorce, keep reminding yourself that leaving your emotionally abusive STBX is an investment in your and your children's future. Any money you spend defending yourself and fighting for freedom and safety can be earned back in the future.

Sitting With the Fear

You're going to need to ignore the opposition and step into the fear— stand toe to toe with it and acknowledge that even though you are afraid you're not going to allow that fear to hold you back. *That* is true strength. You *are* stronger than the fear. Use any fear that comes up to fuel your continued forward progress to get out.

In the next chapter we will discuss the final step in the FREEDOM Framework™ process: Making Your Move. You will learn how to plan your moving day, what you can expect, and other helpful tips so the transition goes as smooth as possible.

Chapter 10

Step 7: Make Your Move

This is it. You've made it to the last step in the FREEDOM Framework™ process and it's moving day! Otherwise known as the first day of your brand-new life.

You probably didn't get much sleep the night before because of all the moving-day plans running through your mind. Despite the pre-planning, it's still going to be a busy day, so allow yourself adequate time to get things situated before your packing buddies show up and the moving truck arrives.

Know that it is completely normal to feel anxious, and you will most likely be running on high adrenaline throughout the day until you are safely out. Be sure to eat a healthy breakfast and drink plenty of fluids throughout the day. If you're unable to eat right away because your stomach is in knots, tuck away a sandwich or snacks to munch on later.

If you spoke to the police previously about your situation and moving out, call them to let them know when the moving truck arrives. Having the police on stand-by will allow them to do drive-by's during the packing and loading process. This will also give you a greater sense of security in knowing they are looking out for you.

Go Dark on Social Media

Sign on to your social media account and block your STBX, and make sure your supporters know in advance not to mention anything about it either. Do *not* post anything, vague or specific, that might tip off your STBX or trigger your friends/followers online to ask questions or make comments. And turn off your GPS, any location tracking apps, and refrain from "checking in" anywhere and posting that to social media.

Regardless of how happy you feel to be free, or how happy your trusted support network is for you, this day and the entire event must be kept off all social media. The airing of any dirty laundry online—by you or your support network—could be used as ammunition by your STBX or his attorney during the divorce process.

You can change your settings in Facebook so others cannot post on your wall, tag you in posts, or send you messages. Doing so for a temporary amount of time will keep the Nosy Nellies from reaching out if they hear rumors in the days following your departure. If you want to be super safe, delete your social media accounts and set up new ones at a later date. Ask your trusted support network to keep an eye out online for anything worrisome posted by others or your STBX.

Getting Started

Have the kids picked up as early as possible for their day of fun. Or, if it's easier, you can have them sleep over at a trusted family member or friend's house the night before, and maybe also the next night, so you have the entire evening to deal with setting up in your new rental.

Once your STBX has departed and your kids have been picked up, it's time to get to work.

The fastest way to complete a "pack, load, and go" move is to make it visually obvious what you want to take. Go through your home and put brightly colored Post-It notes on everything that you plan to take. This includes things in the house (including the basement and attic), garage, and any other storage areas. For larger items, like bigger furniture items, write the room name on the Post-It for where it will go at the new rental, and tape or pin it to the item so it doesn't fall off during the moving process. For kitchens and bathrooms, consider making a list of the items you wish to take—or be in charge of packing those rooms yourself. Designate a packed-box corral area in your garage where boxes can be stacked so they're easily accessible by the movers to immediately load on the truck.

Your primary role will be to facilitate the packing and loading process. Be prepared to answer *lots* of questions from your packing buddies, and you may feel like everyone needs you at once. Focus on one thing at a time and pace yourself.

A safe assumption to tell your packing buddies is that if it looks like you and your kids might need something, they should pack it. You can always return items to your STBX later.

The movers will most likely start loading the boxes first, so it will be ideal for your packing buddies to have everything ready to go when the truck arrives. What they can't finish or what doesn't fit in the truck can be transported in someone else's vehicle.

Packing Buddies

Have your packing buddies show up with their stash of boxes, markers for labeling, packing wrap, and box tape a few hours before the moving truck arrives to help you pack. Ask them to come prepared to work hard and fast. The sooner everything gets packed, the sooner you can safely get out. Designate specific people to work on packing up each room. Have a couple of people work in the kitchen, one be in charge of the bathrooms, another collecting décor from main living areas and off the walls.

Assign a few people to the attic or basement—ideally, people who can handle going up and down steps (or ladders) with boxes. Have a garage-savvy male focus on gathering work tools and supplies you might need in your new place. You can also have them take pictures or video before packing things up, in case you did not have a chance to do that during the research and documentation step. If you cannot put sticky notes on in advance, then make a list for each room of the items you wish to take. Give your packing buddies the list for each room.

Ask that the packed boxes be labeled with the general contents and the room name for the new rental (e.g., "kid toys/ bedroom #2," "mom toiletries/bath #1"). This will help you quickly determine what room each box needs to be delivered to in your new rental.

As soon as a box is filled and labeled, take it to the designated box corral area so the movers can quickly load them into the truck when they arrive.

Load and Go

When the truck arrives, explain to the movers that this is going to be a quick load-and-go move. Have them park as close as they can to the house or garage. Show them where the box corral is located and take them through the house to show them what furniture will be moved. Point out that they should look for the bright Post-It notes to help eliminate any confusion.

While the movers are loading boxes, have your packing buddies start breaking down any beds or furniture that can be dismantled. Use Ziploc bags for keeping screws, nuts, and bolts together, and tape the bag to the item (or label the bag with the name of the piece of furniture and designate one person to hold onto the parts until you get to your new rental).

The movers should be able to wrap dressers with wide plastic rolls so you don't have to box up the drawers' contents.

Go through the house one last time and triple-check that you have everything you need or want, because you will not be coming back. Once everything is packed in the moving truck and your packing buddies' vehicles, send the movers off with a couple of trusted helpers to your new place. Those buddies can open the rental for the movers, show them the rooms and where things will go, and help carry boxes into the new place.

Most movers charge by time, in addition to mileage/distance. To speed up the move-in process, only have the movers carry in the furniture and larger or heavy items. Have the movers unload boxes and stack them in the garage. Your helpers can carry them in to their designated room, storage area, or leave them off to the side. When the truck is empty, the movers will present you with the final bill. If you were pleased with their service and speed with the move, be sure to tip them well.

Saying Good-Bye

You do not need to leave a "Dear John" letter, but if you do—*do not tell him where you went or give him a phone number to call the kids!* The first week after leaving is the most dangerous. If he knows where you are, he could try to take the kids or potentially hurt you. I chose to leave a letter and kept it very brief, telling my STBX that I was sorry to have left in this way, but we could no longer live under the unhealthy conditions, and that I wanted a divorce.

Give yourself adequate time to say good-bye to your home. I did a walk-through, stopping in each room. I said a personal thank-you to the house and asked it to take care of my children, who would be coming back again to visit. The warmth I felt within me as I said my good-bye told me everything was going to be okay and my boys would be safe.

Final Details

Arrange the remaining furniture in the house so your STBX has the basic necessities in each room. Leave your house keys and the garage door opener. Turn off the lights and lock up the house when you leave.

Drive to your new rental to meet up with the movers and your now unpacking buddies.

As soon as you arrive safely at your new rental, notify the police department that you are safely out. In my situation, the sheriff's department waited a few hours until after I was out before they served my STBX with the restraining order at his second job.

You can also request that the law enforcement agency in the place you've moved from notify the police department in your new community that you recently left your abusive spouse, including that you filed a restraining order, if you have. They will provide your STBX's name, a physical description, the type of vehicle he drives, and license plate number. They will likely stop by once you've moved in to touch base with you. At that time, you can ask them to do random drive-by's for a while. They are typically more than happy to oblige.

Settling In

Once the moving truck has left, have your moving buddies unload their vehicles of any items they transported and deliver them to the designated area or room. Similar to when you were packing, have the unpackers assigned to the kitchen, bathrooms, and bedrooms. It's easiest when it's the same person dealing with one area. Have them start putting things away similar to how they were at your former home. Otherwise, if you have time in advance, you can have the cabinets and drawers labeled showing where you want things to go.

If time allows and your helpers are able, start hanging up familiar pictures, put up shelves, and put out other home décor. Set up your kids' rooms similar to how they were before. The more familiar items you have out, the more your new rental will feel comfortable to you and familiar to your kids. I rented a two-bedroom duplex and my boys got to share the larger master bedroom. They had all of their bedroom furniture, bedding, stuffed animals, and toys in place by the time they showed up in their new home, to help it feel more like home.

Letting the Cat Out of the Bag

My young boys were brought to our new rental later in the evening on moving day. They were happy to see my family and friends and thought at first that they were meeting me at someone's house for a birthday party. After most of the unpacking buddies had left, I showed my boys around. I took them into their new bedroom and privately shared the news that we had moved because daddy and I were getting divorced. I told them I was sorry I couldn't tell them before, but I needed to make sure we could get out safely. I assured them that their dad loved them very much, and that they would be able to see him again as soon as the court decided it was okay.

My oldest son took it the hardest. He was seven at the time, and I spent lots of time consoling him and answering his questions. He was very sad and also had anger outbursts when he got frustrated. He did end up going to therapy for a while, where he was able to talk about his sadness and how to self-manage when his anger started ramping up.

My youngest son was only three at the time. He was confused, but he liked that he got to share a bedroom with his big brother. The only odd thing he did was refuse to take his shoes off and he even wanted to wear them to bed for a few weeks, which I allowed.

My parents stayed for a few more hours after everyone else left on moving day, to help me console the boys and get settled in more that night. They came back over the next few days to help me finish unpacking and provide moral support. My trusted support network was great with spending time with my boys, and everyone agreed in advance not to bash my STBX or say anything negative about the situation around the boys, which really helped.

Going forward, focus your attention on helping your kids adjust to the changes and their "new normal," which will more than likely entail living between two homes. Be mindful of your behavior and don't make negative comments about your STBX. This includes not letting them hear you talk on the phone to family or friends about all the drama or divorce proceedings. Continue to create a pleasant and emotionally safe environment for your kids. Also, remember that you are still primarily their parent versus being primarily their friend, so don't allow your guilt to take over, even if they don't like your decisions.

Safety Tips

Statistics show that the most dangerous time for victims of emotional or physical abuse is the point at which they leave the relationship. In addition to what you've already read, it's very important to also consider the following safety tips.

Prepare family and friends—Let them know they might receive calls or texts, or even get a visit from your STBX trying to figure out where you went, and why you stole his kids and everything from the house. Ask them to prepare themselves for a potential confrontation via phone or in person. Have them practice in advance what protective lie they will say, if anything. They also have the choice not to answer the phone or to be conveniently out of town for a while to avoid seeing your STBX. My parents, who lived only a few blocks away from my STBX, stayed at a hotel for the next couple of weeks.

Divorce papers—You can take the lead and have your spouse served with divorce papers, or you can let him have you served. Whoever petitions the divorce pays the filing fees. I got served divorce papers during the restraining order court hearing. My STBX had an attorney at that hearing, but I had not hired one yet. I only had the ladies from the domestic abuse center with me for support. The judge determines whether or not a temporary restraining order will be lifted. Back in 2002, the restraining order I filed was lifted because my STBX never physically hit me. Nowadays, emotional abuse has more leverage in keeping restraining orders in place.

Notify school and daycare—Depending on the time of year you move out, let the school and/or daycare know that you're safely out. If it's a new school or daycare, for the time being (or per your attorney's advice), don't list your STBX on the paperwork until after the initial divorce hearing, when visitation guidelines and parameters are set up and your attorney gives you the okay. You do not want to risk the STBX coming in and taking the kids and creating unnecessary drama before the court can set the appropriate rules each parent is to follow.

Have regular visitors—Invite family and friends over to visit you and your kids so your kids have familiar people around, but remind visitors to be very cautious in the event your STBX tries to follow them, attempting to find you.

Avoid going to your favorite stores to shop or to restaurants alone or with your kids, as your STBX might try to look for you there. Invite family or friends to go with you to stores or restaurants in different communities or areas that your STBX would not normally go to.

Return to work—As soon as you go back to work, confidentially speak to your boss and/or the Human Resource department to update them about your personal situation. Ask for their reasonable flexibility with your schedule in the event court hearings are scheduled during your work shift. Be clear that you will do everything possible for this not to disrupt your work.

Don't be afraid to request a security escort (if available) between work and your vehicle each day until things settle down. If ever on your drive home you get the sense that your STBX is following you, drive directly to a police station. I opted to rent a vehicle the first week back to work so I could travel to and from work more discreetly. I worked at a community college at the time and, for the next couple of weeks, I had the security staff escort me to and from my vehicle each day. That sense of security was priceless.

You can download a handy checklist to help you through the action steps in this chapter by going to www.ijustwantoutbook.com.

YOU MADE IT!

Congratulations on successfully completing your mission! You and your kids made it out safely and are getting settled into your new home. I imagine you are filled with an overwhelming sense of freedom, self-pride, and newfound hope for your future. At the same time you're also wondering what to expect along the next leg of your journey— getting divorced.

The next chapter will provide a general overview of the divorce process in the United States. We'll discuss what you can expect along the way.

Chapter 11

Next Steps

Legal Journey to Freedom

Getting divorced from your emotionally abusive STBX will be a journey of epic proportions. I don't want to frighten you. However, I do want to prepare you for the battle that's likely to occur. As you've been reading throughout the chapters, everything you worked so hard on has been in preparation for this phase of getting the divorce.

While a divorce can be highly emotional and has the potential to become very dramatic, looking at divorce like it's simply the dissolution of a business partnership can help you stay emotionally disconnected so you can look at things more rationally.

If there's one take-away for you from this chapter, I would want it to be this: *Be fair, reasonable, and willing to make concessions.* Regardless of how your STBX treated you and the kids, when it comes to dissolving the business side of the marriage, the above take-away can help you get through the divorce process faster.

Be open to asking yourself, "What is it costing me and my kids to battle over this?" The cost could be financial or emotional, or both.

Being fair and reasonable will also make you look better in the eyes of the court, which could possibly grant you more of what you asked for in the end.

Working With Your Attorney

If you haven't done so already, hire an attorney as soon as possible. Explain your situation and that you moved yourself and your kids out for your safety. Tell him/her if there was a temporary restraining order, and, if so, the outcome of that hearing. Pay them the required retainer and get ready to go to work.

As I mentioned in the last chapter, filing for divorce can be initiated by you or your STBX. Whoever files pays the court filing fees.

Your attorney will have you fill out some basic paperwork and give you a financial disclosure form. This will need to be completed and returned to your attorney prior to the initial or pre-trial hearing. He/she will give you a deadline to have it completed and returned so they can review it and make any necessary adjustments. This is where *all* your hard work during the previous steps will pay off.

Gather all of the documentation (original paperwork, copies, and anything electronic) for your financials, both assets and debts, so you can complete the financial disclosure form. There may be a lot of paperwork to sort through, so be sure to allow yourself adequate time to complete this, and do not hesitate to recruit a trusted family member or friend to assist you.

Disclose *everything* financially to your attorney, even if it doesn't look ideal on your end. If you cashed out an IRA before leaving and that means you will be hit with a big tax penalty, share that detail anyway. The only upside to cashing things out is that you prevent your spouse from having access to half of what was earned in your account during your marriage. However, the court could hold you fully liable to pay the penalty fees. Know that if the court deems that cashing out retirement funds or creating excessive debt was done maliciously, you could end up with that debt.

You have the option of giving all of the unsorted paperwork to your attorney for him/her to sort out, but that would waste a great deal of their time and cost you a large portion of the retainer fee you just paid.

Manage Your Divorce

Attorneys rely on their clients to help keep them on track. Do *not* expect him/her to run the entire show. If you take a backseat in your divorce it could potentially cost you more money and may negatively impact what you're awarded in the end. Do *not* assume your attorney will keep every detail straight with your divorce; you are *not* his/her only client. You may need to remind him/her of details as you go along, and do not be afraid to follow-up on items you discussed if you haven't heard a response in a timely fashion.

When speaking with your attorney, stick to the matters at hand. As I stated at the beginning of this chapter, getting divorced can be highly emotional and traumatic, but your job is to keep your emotions to a minimum as much as possible when speaking and corresponding with your attorney. They are not your coach or therapist, and they will charge you for *every* minute of their time, so sharing anything you don't need to will result in burning through your retainer more quickly. Obviously, if there is an issue that arises that's very unsettling, please notify your attorney.

Monitor your retainer balance. Once it is depleted, request to go on a payment plan for the duration of your divorce process. Some attorneys may temporarily cease working your case if you don't keep up on your monthly payments.

Most of your communication with your attorney can take place via email, but that is not always the best mode, as things could end up getting confused and take longer to sort out. Upon hiring your attorney, ask about their preferred mode of communication. Whether they prefer to meet in person or prefer phone calls, find out what you will be charged for that time. You may wish to schedule weekly or biweekly calls so that you can keep the calls focused, and to have a regular time to touch base and discuss any detailed matters. To save money, email your attorney with updates or new information. Group multiple topics in one email so your messages don't get lost easily in his/her inbox.

To help you stay organized, consider purchasing a large binder or an inexpensive two-drawer file cabinet to store physical divorce process documents. Set up hanging files or tabs to keep paperwork and correspondence organized. Having a place to put this information will keep it safe from getting accidentally misplaced or thrown away. Keep your emails organized as well. Give your attorney your secret email address and create a folder to move electronic correspondence into once you've attended to it.

I started with a binder and then expanded to a two-drawer file cabinet. I found it beneficial to have a place to quickly tuck away paperwork and letters so my kids wouldn't risk seeing them and get worried. Plus, when my kids were with me and I didn't need to focus on my divorce proceedings, I could simply close up the file drawer and shift my attention to other, more enjoyable things.

Initial Pre-Trial Hearing

Plan to have an in-person meeting or phone session with your attorney a few days before the initial pre-trial hearing, to discuss the financial disclosure form and any other matters. Divulge *everything* you know that's pertinent to your divorce, and be completely honest and transparent with your attorney, as this will help build trust and respect with him/her faster. Seriously, do not hide anything, even if you think it doesn't look favorably upon you. I assure you, attorneys have first-hand experience with such issues, or have heard worse situations than what you'll ever present.

After hiring my attorney, an initial hearing was scheduled with the family court commissioner. That individual is an attorney appointed by the court to review the financial disclosure form and other pertinent details, which helps them make determinations for a temporary order, which includes issues such as: child custody and placement arrangements (who has primary placement of the kids); visitation (when the kids get to see and/or be with the other parent); child support payments; who is responsible for paying which bills, etc. This is also where the court will ask you to give your new phone number (cell phone or landline) to your STBX so he can call his children.

When you go for the initial hearing, or any court proceedings for that matter, it is in your best interest to go in with an open mind and the stance of being fair and reasonable. If you go into court expecting or demanding to have it all your way and not compromise, you will learn it rarely works out that way. In addition, if you present yourself as highly emotional or unstable, or display immature behavior in court— glaring at your STBX or his attorney, answering questions in a snappy tone, losing your temper, rolling your eyes, reactively whispering to your attorney—you will not represent yourself well, which could impact how you are perceived by the court and possibly affect what extras you are awarded at the final divorce hearing.

Kid Expenses

Keep a running log of any expenses you incur for the kids during the divorce process, such as for medical or dental care, daycare or after-school care, school registration fees and school supplies, clothing expenses, etc. Discuss with your attorney what items are to be split 50/50 with your STBX. If your STBX has to pay child support per the temporary order, do not be surprised to hear your STBX say that child support should cover all of the kids' expenses. Do not argue; rather, turn the matter over to your attorney to discuss with your STBX's attorney.

I sent my STBX monthly emails with scanned copies of paid bills and receipts, and I included an Excel spreadsheet detailing each of the items, the total, and our respective responsible amounts. I also copied my attorney in those emails.

Today, however, there are much handier communication apps and online calendars available, such as Our Family Wizard (which charges a fee and offers multiple logins) and Cozi (free), that can be used by divorcing and post-divorce couples to communicate schedules (for kids and parents), set up child exchanges, and log variable expenses and reimbursements.

It's common for reimbursements to be made within 30 days of receipt. Any significant amounts your STBX is in arrears by at the time of the final hearing can be added to a payout settlement or possibly garnished from his employment wages or his next tax return.

Communications With Stbx

The initial or pre-trial hearing is probably the first time you will see your STBX since moving out. His demeanor will most likely be combatant and he will behave in an argumentative manner. Do not be surprised if he takes this as an opportunity to bash you in front of the court, calling you names and stating that you stole the kids, his things, and maybe even his money. His primary goal is to punish you and demand that you get nothing, because it's all his. Let him rattle off whatever nastiness he wants, but do not react or respond. Stare off into the distance and tune him out. Remember that you're used to being put down and treated like you're "less than" by him, so this should come as no surprise. Let your STBX dig his own hole throughout this divorce process.

If you must communicate with your STBX, do so via email or text. That way you have written proof of his behavior and comments he makes toward you or about the kids during the divorce process. You can also share these exchanges with your attorney.

When your STBX first calls to speak to the kids, layout the ground rules and stand firm to them. This is not the time to get wishy-washy, as he will use that as an opportunity to attack you or try to bait you into an argument. Keep being the ice queen.

If you must speak to your STBX, do not engage in any arguing banter. Focus only on the facts or details about the kids, and nothing else. If he verbally threatens you or the kids, or sends threatening messages, hang up and inform your attorney right away. He/she will assess the matter and take appropriate action if necessary.

Tell your STBX that he is only allowed to call at specific times to speak to the kids (give him times that are reasonable), and he is not allowed to speak with the kids about anything pertaining to you or the divorce proceedings, which are off limits. Advise him that you will be monitoring the calls via speakerphone and any talk of him blaming Mommy or asking the kids to give him information will result in the call ending. In addition, tell him you will only speak with him on matters pertaining to the children. Any details regarding the divorce will be communicated and hashed out between the attorneys. Be prepared for him *not* to comply with the ground rules when he calls, or *not* to reciprocate when the kids are with him and you call. You can hang up the phone rather than tolerate him not complying with the rules you've set.

Be on the lookout as he may also try to bargain and offer false promises that he'll stop addictive habits, drop expensive hobbies, or quit a second job if that's what'll make you happy and you'll come home, or if that will stop all this unnecessary craziness you've created. Simply tell him, "No thanks," and give the phone to your kids to have their conversation, or end the call. His false promises are only ploys to get you back, in private, so he can put you in your place, abuse you more, and potentially hurt or attempt to kill you. Do not put that past your STBX! You have successfully pulled the rug out from beneath him by being cunning and strategic, and he's furious with you.

Do not agree to meet your STBX anywhere with the kids before or in-between his assigned visitations, despite how much he begs to see them. He may struggle with this, but he will adjust and get used to it. That behavior will end as soon as he comes up with a new retaliation tactic.

Continue to let your STBX know about school or daycare activities or programs where parents are invited so he can be involved with the kids. He will likely behave himself in public, but you'd do better to still have your kids say their good-byes while you're in the building around other people.

Child Exchanges and Drop-Offs

Have your attorney request from the court that any child exchanges (pick-ups and drop-offs) happen in a public place, preferably where there are video surveillance cameras. It can be at a respectable convenience store, or a McDonald's or other fast-food restaurant parking lot. Be sure to park close to the building and within camera range so the exchange gets recorded. If there's a police station nearby, don't hesitate to request to have the exchange in their parking lot instead.

Do not do child exchanges at your house or his or where nobody can witness what's going on. If exchanges are done in non-public areas this will be your STBX's opportunity to dole out his threats at you, and he will not hesitate to do it in front of the kids. Do not give him the opportunity to get you alone! Be prepared for backlash from your STBX when you don't comply with his demands. This could include new threats that he'll take you down and make you pay, harm you physically, get you fired from your job, make everyone turn against you, get the kids back, or make sure you'll never see the kids again. Relay any verbal threats to your attorney. If your STBX threatens to physically harm you or your kids, call 911 immediately and follow-up with your attorney later.

Mediation

The court may require that divorcing couples attend mediation to try to sort through any of the financials, personal property, and marital property, such as the house or land. The court has mediators staffed to help facilitate the meetings, and those people know nothing about the details of your situation until they meet you. Be prepared for your STBX to take this as an opportunity to try to turn the mediator against you. He may cast blame at you for tearing the family apart, accuse you of being crazy, or even say that you're brainwashing the kids. The mediator may try to get the meeting back on topic, but your STBX will not agree to let you have anything.

The mediation session I attended with my ex resulted in him shaming me, verbally tearing me down, and telling me I did not deserve anything, because I was evil for stealing his kids and his stuff. After 15 minutes I'd had enough. I apologized to the mediator, said I couldn't do this, and walked out. My exit frustrated my attorney, but I later explained that I knew nothing was going to get resolved in there and I wasn't willing to let myself be treated like that just to please the court. The upside is that the mediator documented what happened and that got turned over to the court, and it ultimately gave merit to my claims of emotional abuse.

Custody Study

Depending on the state and county you live in, the court may appoint a guardian ad litem (GAL) to perform a custody study. This is an attorney assigned to represent the children in the divorce. They determine what's in the kids' best interest as it pertains to custody and placement matters. The GAL does *not* work for you or your STBX. Don't try to steer their decision in any way by kissing their butt or trying to intimidate them. Your job is to meet with the GAL, most likely at your home, show them around your home, and let him/her interview the kids privately. The GAL may wish to interview family members on both sides as well. In some situations, there may be a trial and witnesses called to testify.

Before meeting with the GAL, take some time to research child-placement options online. There are many free and paid websites and apps that you can access to help calculate and track child custody (aka, placement or overnights) and child support.

Next, think about your STBX and what you feel (and know) he'll be able to handle as far as visitation and overnights. Is he able to help the kids with their homework? Get them reliably to their extra-curricular activities or sports? Can he handle parenting the kids? Will he spend time with them? Does he even know how to take care of them?

I want you to envision the kids with their dad every other week, or every other weekend with a mid-week visitation (either for a few hours or overnight), and I want you to envision holidays without your children. This is not to upset you, but rather prepare you for what may lie ahead for you and your children. Some states and counties have reputations for awarding 50/50 placement, regardless of the dad's behavior.

Take adequate time to seriously think about and get clear about when you might want to not have your kids. This is not about being uncaring, unmotherly, or selfish, but it's definitely something to consider.

The placement you get awarded may affect your ability to change jobs, get a second job if you'd like, or even start school.

Despite everything that's happened, your kids do deserve to still have a relationship with their dad and sincerely share that with the GAL. You can offer suggestions about visitation arrangements that you feel are in the kids' best interests and that fit with what you want or need. Do not go into the meeting with the GAL with an agenda where you want to have the kids more so you can get more child support. GALs can see right through that garbage and you could potentially end up with little or no visitation, lose primary placement, or receive less child support.

When the GAL visited my new home and interviewed me and then the kids, he was very respectful. He spent time really observing my kids' behaviors with me. I told him about my marriage, how I had been affected, and how the kids had been starting to be the target of their dad's anger and put-downs. I spoke honestly about my concerns and the negative impact my STBX's behavior had had on the kids' overall well-being.

I also shared my opinions about when I felt my STBX could best manage having the kids in addition to working his full-time and part-time jobs. I proposed that he get the kids for longer visitation during the summer months—one full week each month—in addition to his normal Wednesday overnights, every other weekend, and rotating holidays. The GAL didn't give me a response during our meeting, but during the final court hearing he presented the exact visitation schedule I recommended.

Every custody study is different and the results can vary. The key is to be open with the GAL. They have your kids' best interests in mind.

Investigation Phase

The main phase of the divorce process is commonly referred to as the "investigation phase." This is when the majority of the details are discussed and negotiated between the attorneys. Hopefully, both attorneys can get along and work things out fairly, but if one is a barracuda type, they will want to engage in nasty letter-writing campaigns to try to shake you up, in hopes that you will cave and accept less than you're entitled to. Those are only scare tactics, so try not to take them personally. Your STBX will be paying a lot of money to his attorney for unnecessary letter-writing time. Your attorney should only respond to the topics that are pertinent to the divorce or on matters that you agree need to be addressed.

Additional things that may come up during the investigation phase include having a formal accounting of personal property, as well as getting a mental health evaluation (if it was not already included in the custody study). Being aware of the potential requirements listed below may help reduce your emotional reactions and better prepare you should they be necessary.

Personal Property Appraisal—Your STBX may allege that you stole all of his stuff, but the attorneys will most likely want an appraiser to help them determine the value of the personal property at each residence. The appraiser is an independent representative and does not work on behalf of either attorney. He/she will need a list of contents from both parties, and then will call to schedule an appointment to meet with you to view the items listed and determine a value. If there are items on loan from family or friends, be sure to make mention of that in advance, so they're not accidentally included in the overall appraisal.

In my case, I had my attorney forward the original home inventory I had created and what items I took along when I moved. Being prepared worked in my favor when it came to the financial split of assets and the payout I was awarded at the final divorce hearing.

Psychiatric Evaluation—As you read in the first two chapters, I shared that I had spent time in therapy. Depending on the depth of your STBX's distortion campaign and the determination of the custody study, you may be ordered to have a psych evaluation. The psych evaluation is typically paid in advance and today can cost anywhere from $1,000 to

$3,000. You can expect to spend a few hours at the appointment being evaluated by the shrink and also taking an extensive personality test. It's normal to feel stressed out before and during the appointment, and even afterwards to worry about the worst-case outcomes.

It seems ridiculous in many ways, but after having to go through a psych evaluation I believe it benefited the outcome of my divorce. The report from the doctor said that I was a "ruminator," and my STBX was found to have "severe mother issues" (no kidding—his mother was crazy and he had an awful childhood). The psych evaluation did not negatively affect the percentage of child placement or the amount of child support I received, like my STBX had hoped. The court awarded me primary placement of the children and substantial child support.

Negotiation Phase

The attorneys will use basic templates and formulas for figuring out placement, visitation, holiday rotation, child support, division of assets and debts, as well as whether a financial settlement is to be awarded. Whenever possible, provide proposals to your attorney and consider fair and reasonable proposals from the other attorney. Do not overlook visitation for special dates, such as birthdays (yours, STBX's, and the kids'), Mother's Day and Father's Day, family traditions (vacation times), religious events, and holidays.

In my situation, we rotated most of the major holidays using the standard schedule provided by the attorneys. Christmas Eve and Christmas Day were split and rotated. My kids were always with me for Mother's Day and my birthday, and were always with their dad for his special days, but we chose not to rotate the kids' birthdays, as they did not take place during holidays or in the summer. However, you may wish to rotate the kids' birthdays. To avoid issues with the start of each school year, I got the boys every Labor Day weekend and, in exchange, they were always with their dad for Memorial Day weekend.

If you qualify to receive child support, your attorney will most likely calculate it first based on placement (e.g., total number of overnights), income levels and differences, and what he thinks the judge might deem as fair in the case.

This phase also includes figuring out other details regarding the kids and what will be put into the final divorce decree. Typically, medical and dental expenses are split 50/50. Daycare and after-school care expenses can be split 50/50 or by a percentage based on placement or income differences. Tax deductions are usually split so that each parent gets a child, and when the oldest "ages out" (usually, when they turn 18), then the deductions are taken in alternate years. Or if there's an odd number of dependents, the youngest alternates until the older children age out.

In my situation, we split the kids' medical and dental costs 50/50. But daycare expenses were split according to the placement I was awarded, which was 60/40. I paid 60 percent of the daycare bills.

Items that can be easily overlooked are variable expenses, such as school registration fees, school lunch, school supplies, sports fees, uniforms or equipment, band instruments, class trips, cell phones, and—when they get older—automobile insurance. Even if your children are very young, request that auto insurance coverage be written into the final paperwork. You can split that expense 50/50 or have each parent insure a child. Having these *small* details addressed up-front may seem petty or a waste of time, but I assure you that when your child turns 16 and gets his or her driver's license you'll appreciate having *that* expensive detail figured out in advance. Plus, it can potentially reduce the need to return to court years down the road to fight for financial assistance or reimbursement.

I did not have variable expenses detailed in my final divorce, mainly because my attorney said that stuff could be addressed later. I had no idea at the time what a hassle it would be trying to get my ex to help out and hearing him say, "That's what I already pay child support for." I ended up providing a vehicle and the insurance for my oldest son. I went back to court after my youngest turned 16, to address the auto insurance and a variety of other unresolved financial matters, but the court ruled that my ex had to split the insurance expense with me 50/50 versus requiring him to cover all of it.

Finally, as it pertains to child support and splitting expenses for the children, be sure it's stated that the arrangement continues until that child graduates from high school, or turns 18, whichever comes later.

Bargaining Chips

Bargaining chips are the other "asset" details you get to negotiate. These things can vary greatly and are different in every divorce. Earlier in the book, you were tasked with researching the balances of all your retirement accounts. You may be eligible to half of the amount that was earned in your STBX's fund for the duration of your marriage.

If you are entitled to half of your STBX's retirement, you can decide whether that's something you even want. Look at your overall situation and discuss it with your attorney. A great way to show you're being fair and reasonable is to offer, early on, that you do not want any of his retirement money. The fact is, you cannot access that money until after you've retired. If you want to fully disconnect from your abusive spouse, disconnecting from his money will help.

Depending on how long you've been married and whether there's a significant difference in your incomes, you may be eligible to receive "maintenance," which is commonly referred to as "alimony." Each state can calculate maintenance differently, but it usually is only awarded to extend for a length of time after the divorce that is equivalent to half of the length of your marriage. Discuss this with your attorney, but if you can honestly afford to go without it, then do so. The primary reason is, again, to fully disconnect from your STBX. In addition, you would have to claim maintenance as income on your taxes, and your ex gets to deduct it from his. Turning down maintenance is another way to show the court you are being fair and reasonable. The court may respond more favorably to you on child support issues or the division of other financial matters if you decline maintenance. Obviously, if you qualify for it and need it to financially survive, due to income differences or other reasons, then please do not turn it down.

I was married for eleven years and chose to decline maintenance. I would have only received around $125.00 per month, and it honestly didn't seem worth it to me. Plus, I didn't want to have to rely on STBX's money. I also declined half of his retirement fund, because our balances were similar. If I had gone for his, then he would have gone for mine, which seemed like a waste of time and energy for no appreciable outcome.

Final Divorce Hearing

If the attorneys cannot come to agreement by the scheduled final divorce hearing, a trial will occur. Most times, there is no jury and it's a matter of the attorneys presenting their findings and any already-agreed-upon determinations. The lingering items that could not be settled will go before the judge for determination. Each party will take the stand and can be questioned by each attorney or only the judge. Once the outstanding matters are settled, the judge will then review what has been agreed upon and double-check that there are no unaddressed objections.

The GAL is also in attendance at the trial and presents his/ her formal determination from the custody study to the court, regarding child custody, primary placement, and visitation. In advance of the final hearing, the GAL typically shares their determination with the attorneys, so they can create visitation and holiday rotation schedules for each party to follow.

When everything has been presented, discussed, and agreed upon, the judge will make a final ruling and grant the divorce.

Post-Divorce

Once you're legally divorced, it takes time for the heated emotions to settle on both sides. Keep conversations with your ex to only matters that pertain to the kids. There will still be things the attorneys will need to get wrapped up, like adjustments to child support, typing up the final documents for the judge to sign, having you sign over deeds or titles to any marital property your ex is keeping, and paperwork if you're going to receive a settlement in the divorce from your ex. In that event, your ex gets time to refinance the mortgage into only his name and to come up with the money to pay you out. That money is usually sent first to your ex's attorney and then to your attorney. Your attorney will then deduct any unpaid legal fees and, finally, send you a check for the remaining balance.

The Aftermath

After the court has ruled and the ink on the divorce paperwork has dried, you may feel elated to finally be free, but you also may feel a bit numb and lost for a while. That's normal and completely understandable.

This is a great time to help yourself process through the big changes you've been working toward and have now accomplished. You can do this by shifting your focus away from your ex-husband and all the administration of getting through the divorce proceedings, to focus instead on reassessing the state of your own needs.

Take some time to really think about what things you've wanted to do, see, experience, and have. Make a wish list or create a dream board in Pinterest, or get really hands-on and make your very own vision board using magazine clippings of pictures and words or phrases that represent things you want for yourself. You can even make a separate one for your children—things you want to be able to do with them or possibly provide for them. Your wish list or boards can contain things from the simple and practical to the challenging and exciting to the hopeful and dreamy, and include ideas you'd love to achieve within the next five to ten years. Hang it up in full view—on your bedroom wall, by your bathroom mirror, or on the refrigerator door—where you will see it often and so it can help you manifest your various dreams.

Things you can consider starting now on a divorce recovery level include ramping up your fitness routine, spending more time with friends and family, taking down-time for yourself (to read, get a massage, or watch a show), meeting new people, and getting settled into your new home and community.

If you've wanted to exercise more, join a fitness center where you can work out or take group classes, or recruit a friend to be your walking buddy. You can turn your attention to learning new hobbies (cooking, painting, making pottery, or crafting) and other fun activities (joining a book club, running in 5ks, hiking, kayaking, or paddle boarding). There are a wide variety of classes available or meet-up groups you could join. If you getting to know your community and becoming more involved interests you, you can volunteer to help out at local events, join a new church, or organize a neighborhood block party. And if you're in need of additional emotional support to help you recover, seek out a divorce support group (such as Divorce Care) or a group specific to emotional abuse recovery. Such groups are often offered by mental health clinics, churches, or nonprofit organizations.

This, my dear, is a great opportunity to get to know yourself— who you *really* are—as you begin to live your brand-new, beautiful, and free life!

You can download a handy checklist to help you through the action steps in this chapter by going to www.ijustwantoutbook.com.

Chapter 12

Recaps And Reminders

Here we are at the conclusion of your voyage. We've walked through the story of my awakening and realization that I was in an emotionally abusive marriage. We discussed that your journey to freedom is a gain, not a loss, and we went through each of the detailed steps of the *FREEDOM Framework™* process. You learned how to plan and safely execute your move, what to expect along the way, and about the general divorce process.

My wish for you is that this book has offered inspiration and provided answers to your questions (even to ones you may not have even thought of), has filled you with hope, and has given you the strength to leave your abusive marriage so you can have a better—no, scratch that—an *amazing* future!

Where I Am Today

As of the publishing date of this book, nearly 15 years have passed since my boys and I left my abusive husband. I am long recovered from the emotional abuse and trauma I experienced in that first marriage.

Because of all the standing up I did to get out of that abusive marriage, *I changed*. I changed enough to want a lot more for myself and to understand a lot more about what makes a relationship healthy. I gave myself permission to be divorced and explore life. I focused on my kids and their needs. I traveled, went back to school, built new friendships, and strengthened relationships with loved ones. I also allowed myself to date different types of men and to learn what qualities were and weren't a good fit for me. It wasn't all easy-peasy; it was messy and involved lots of trial and error. Yet, through it all, I kept moving forward.

My boys have also recovered. They have grown into emotionally healthy, respectable, decent young men. They made wonderful new friends after our move, did well in school, and enjoyed participating in sports and extracurricular activities.

The three of us have had many fun adventures and have created wonderful memories together. My older son is in his junior year of college, studying kinesiology, and plans to continue on to graduate school. My younger son is nearing the end of high school and is interested in studying psychology. That's pretty cool, considering that some of the people who harshly judged me years ago told me my boys wouldn't amount to anything. I felt very confident back in 2002 when I heard those comments and I still feel confident today in saying that they were dead wrong.

A few days after my 40th birthday, I went on a blind date and met a man who would become my best friend and the love of my life, Dan. He had a spark about him that I couldn't forget, and he possessed *all* of the important things I had been looking for in a life partner. We were married on February 13, 2013, during a sunset ceremony on a beautiful beach in Hawaii.

Since I met Dan, he has been my beacon if ever I feel lost, my sounding board when I need to vent or want advice, my cheerleader who always encourages me, my rock supporting me as I continue to pursue my dreams, and he's a great friend and positive role model for my boys.

While what I endured during my first marriage was painful, it taught me so many beneficial lessons. From that experience, I learned:

- About myself—how to trust my intuition and my strength; how much I can handle; that I am smart and know what to do; and my level of perseverance.
- About my children—how to be present for them; how to be their primary emotional support; how to teach them to be more self-aware; how to best encourage them when they're feeling down; and how to model healthy behavior.
- About relationships—what's healthy and what's unhealthy (including with friends and family); and how not to allow fear to hold me back or dictate my dreams and happiness.

I went on to pursue my academic goal of earning a master's degree. I left corporate America and enjoyed teaching and training in colleges. Now I'm a Certified Life Coach who specializes in relationships and helping to make a difference in other people's lives. I am so proud to have the ability to share my experience and to support other women through the empowering and life-changing process of getting a divorce as a journey to freedom.

Continue Your Journey With Me

As you've read this book, there may have been others who came to mind that you feel could also benefit from my story and my experience. I invite you to share this book with them.

You can visit www.ijustwantoutbook.com to download all the checklists to help keep you on track as you complete the FREEDOM Framework™ process.

If you would like an experienced companion to walk beside you on your journey to freedom, you can apply for my Six Weeks to Freedom program. You'll find details on my website: www.ijustwantoutbook.com.

I wish you strength and hope, and send you love and light.

Acknowledgments

I want to start by thanking my entire family for always standing by me, even if they disagreed or didn't understand. And, for being open-minded and willing to learn from my life experiences. I appreciate them for all the joy and great memories they help create when we're all together.

Thanks to my parents for not stopping after three children—or four, for that matter! To my dad for all of his unconditional love, and to my mom for always pushing me to learn and advance myself. Thanks to both of them for showing me what hard work looks like, and for always being willing to help out.

I am grateful to my sisters, my brother, and brothers-in-law for encouraging me to find myself and to look at the world through a bigger lens. And for showing me how to step into my fears, trust the process, and stand up for myself unapologetically.

I'd like to also thank both my former therapist, Kelly, and my former coworker, Jeff, for helping me safely navigate the scary predivorce waters. Their unrelenting support and guidance has never been forgotten and paved the way for me to help and support others.

Thanks to all my dear friends who helped and who provided moral support throughout my leaving process, as well as during my divorce—they know who they are! Thanks also to my inner circle of friends who've watched me transform from caterpillar to butterfly multiple times over. And thanks to the many friends I've made post-divorce—I'm grateful for their continued kindness, love, and support.

I have a deep appreciation for my fellow MBI tribe mates who stepped forward to share their experiences of leaving their abusive spouses. I'm thankful to them for offering their successes and mistakes so I could provide additional details for my readers to help them better plan and execute their own departures.

Thanks to my husband Dan and my boys for their unconditional love and for teaching me new things everyday about life through their knowledge and experiences. Also, for being authentic, fun, and for supporting my passion of making a difference in the world.

I appreciate the entire crew at The Author Incubator for their professionalism, support, and belief in helping authors fulfill their dreams. Thanks to Angela Lauria for speaking directly to me through her video and book, and for helping me evolve through her amazing program so I can help others. And a special thanks to my managing editor, Grace Kerina, for all of her support and suggestions, and especially for being my wordsmith—all while retaining *my* voice.

Thank you to my divorce attorney, Keith, for taking on my case and going to bat for me countless times during and after my divorce. His patience, understanding, and encouragement helped me greatly during a very scary and stressful time in my life. His approach of always first telling me the worst-case scenario scared the hell out of me, but I came to appreciate it because he was adamant about being realistic. I especially appreciated that things, therefore, always turned out for the better. Thanks as well to him for being my *legal eagle* in regard to this book.

I am eternally grateful for the countless clients I've had the pleasure of coaching, who had the courage to face their fears and allow me to walk alongside them during their transformations.

About the Author

Jodi Schuelke's essential belief is that women who learn to listen to and trust their intuition experience more freedom and joy in their life. She is passionate about helping women reclaim their strength, open up new ways of thinking, and discover breakthroughs so they can move on from relationships that are no longer serving them to a happier and healthier life.

She is an adept relationship coach who also has many years of first-hand experience: 10 years spent trying to *fix* her emotionally abusive first marriage, going through a divorce, co-parenting, enduring a tumultuous rebound relationship and break-up, dating in her mid-thirties, journeying to find Mr. Right, and getting married again.

Jodi has a master's degree in management and organizational behavior, with an emphasis in training and development. After fifteen years working in corporate America, she changed her career to teaching business and communications courses at the college level. Jodi also began facilitating corporate training workshops in change management, leadership, sales and customer service that also included providing professional coaching sessions to corporate clients. That experience paved the way for obtaining life coach certification from the Martha Beck Institute. Today Jodi enjoys providing relationship coaching to individuals and small groups.

She lives in northeast Wisconsin with her husband, Dan, her two sons and step-children, and a fur-child, Echo the Siberian Husky.

Thank You!

Hey, thanks for reading *I Just Want Out*. This isn't the end, but rather the beginning of a life-changing and worthwhile future. I sincerely hope this book has provided you with peace of mind and encouragement as you plan your departure and your divorce.

Download The Free Checklists

Please visit my website to download helpful free checklists to keep you on track as you complete the FREEDOM Framework™ process: www. ijustwantoutbook.com.

Start Your Journey To Freedom

If you would like an experienced companion to walk beside you on your journey to freedom, you can apply for my Six Weeks to Freedom program. You'll find details on my website: www.ijustwantoutbook.com.